YOUR recipe could appear in our next cookbook!

T0044682

Share your tried & true family favorites with us instantly at

www.gooseberrypatch.com

If you'd rather jot 'em down by hand, just mail this form to...

Gooseberry Patch • Cookbooks – Call for Recipes
PO Box 812 • Columbus, OH 43216-0812

If your recipe is selected for a book, you'll receive a FREE copy!

Please share only your original recipes or those that you have made your own over the years.

Recipe Name:

Number of Servings:

Any fond memories about this recipe? Special touches you like to add
or handy shortcuts?

Ingredients (include specific measurements):

Instructions (continue on back if needed):

Special Code: **cookbookspage**

Over ➤

Extra space for recipe if needed:

Tell us about yourself...

Your complete contact information is needed so that we can send you your FREE cookbook, if your recipe is published. Phone numbers and email addresses are kept private and will only be used if we have questions about your recipe.

Name:

Address:

City: State: Zip:

Email:

Daytime Phone:

Thank you! Vickie & Jo Ann

Harvest for Sharing

A bountiful harvest of scrumptious recipes, plus
fall fun in the country with family & friends.

Gooseberry Patch

An imprint of Globe Pequot
64 South Main Street
Essex, CT 06426

www.gooseberrypatch.com

1•800•854•6673

Copyright 2024, Gooseberry Patch 978-1-62093-569-9

Do you have a tried & true recipe...

tip, craft or memory that you'd like to see featured in
a **Gooseberry Patch** cookbook? Visit our website at
www.gooseberrypatch.com and follow the
easy steps to submit your favorite family recipe.
Or send them to us at:

Gooseberry Patch
PO Box 812
Columbus, OH 43216-0812

Don't forget to include the number of servings your recipe makes,
plus your name, address, phone number and email address. If we
select your recipe, your name will appear right along with it...
and you'll receive a **FREE** copy of the book!

Contents

Cozy Breakfasts for Sharing 5

Favorite Sides & Salads 37

Warm & Inviting Soups 71

Feasts for Family & Friends.............. 105

Tailgate Get-Togethers 145

Scrumptious Cookies & Desserts........179

Dedication

Dedicated to everyone who loves watching the leaves change color, choosing the biggest pumpkin and sharing the best of times with family & friends.

Appreciation

To our family & friends...thank you for sharing your most delicious fall recipes.

Cozy
Breakfasts
for Sharing

Harvest
for Sharing

Mom's Sweet Potato Waffles

Paula Marchesi
Auburn, PA

*I enjoy making a delicious breakfast for family & friends. This recipe
is really easy and easy to double, too. I've even made this
using cooked pumpkin and butternut squash.*

1-1/2 c. sweet potatoes, peeled
   and quartered
3 eggs, separated
1-1/2 c. milk
1/3 c. brown sugar, packed
1/4 c. butter, melted

2 c. all-purpose flour
1 T. baking powder
2 t. cinnamon
1 t. salt
Garnish: cinnamon-sugar,
   maple syrup

In a saucepan, cover sweet potatoes with water. Cook over high heat
until fork-tender; drain. Add sweet potatoes to a large bowl and mash.
Add egg yolks, milk, brown sugar and melted butter; whisk well and
set aside. In another large bowl, whisk together flour, baking powder,
cinnamon and salt. Add sweet potato mixture to flour mixture and
whisk until smooth; batter will be thick. In a small bowl, beat egg
whites with an electric mixer on high speed until stiff peaks form.
With a spatula, gently fold egg whites into batter. Ladle batter by
1/2 to 3/4 cupfuls onto a preheated, greased waffle iron; cook
according to manufacturer's instructions. Serve waffles topped with
cinnamon-sugar and maple syrup. Makes 10 small waffles.

Watch for old-fashioned syrup or cream pitchers at tag sales...
set out a variety of sweet toppings like flavored syrups and
honey for fluffy pancakes and waffles.

Cozy Breakfasts
for Sharing

Coffee Shop Egg Bites

Hannah Stoltzfus
Denver, PA

This is one of our favorite brunch recipes. These tasty morsels are easy to freeze and reheat for quick breakfasts on busy days, too.

5 eggs
1 c. cottage cheese
1 c. shredded Swiss cheese
1/8 t. salt

1/8 t. pepper
2 slices bacon, crisply cooked
    and crumbled

Combine eggs and cottage cheese in in a blender; process until smooth. Pour into a bowl; stir in Swiss cheese, salt and pepper. Pour mixture into 12 greased muffin cups, filling 1/2 full. Top with crumbled bacon. Bake, uncovered, at 350 degrees for 30 minutes, or until eggs are set. Remove from oven; turn out of pan and serve warm. Makes one dozen.

Small-town county fairs, food festivals, craft shows, swap meets...the list goes on & on, so grab a friend or two and go for good old-fashioned fun! A hearty warm breakfast will get you off to a terrific start.

Harvest
for Sharing

Aunt Carol's Sour Cream Coffee Cake

Karen Gierhart
Fremont, OH

My aunt gave me this delicious recipe years ago. She passed away a few years ago...I think of her every time I make it.

3/4 c. butter, softened
1-1/2 c. sugar
1 c. sour cream
2 eggs, beaten
1 t. vanilla extract
2 c. all-purpose flour

1 t. baking powder
1/2 t. salt
2/3 c. chopped walnuts
1/4 c. light brown sugar, packed
2 t. baking cocoa
1 t. cinnamon

Blend together butter and sugar in a large bowl. Add sour cream, eggs and vanilla; mix well. Add flour, baking powder and salt; stir well and set aside. For topping, mix together remaining ingredients in a small bowl. Spoon half of batter into a greased angel food cake pan; sprinkle with half of topping. Repeat layering. Bake at 350 degrees for 50 minutes. Cool in pan for 20 minutes; turn out onto a plate. If desired, drizzle with Glaze; slice and serve. Makes 12 servings.

Glaze:

1-1/2 c. powdered sugar
2 to 3 drops vanilla extract

2 T. milk

Mix together all ingredients, adding enough milk for a glaze consistency.

Invite an old friend, or the new neighbor you've been wanting to get to know better, to share coffee cake and the latest news...you'll be so glad you did!

Cozy Breakfasts
for Sharing

Tex-Mex Egg & Potato Skillet

Angela Murphy
Tempe, AZ

This hearty breakfast is perfect on game-day mornings!

3 T. oil, divided
20-oz. pkg. refrigerated
    southwest-style shredded
    hashbrowns
1 c. red pepper, diced
1 T. butter

10 eggs, beaten
1/4 c. fresh cilantro or
    parsley, chopped
1 c. shredded Monterey
    Jack cheese
Garnish: salsa, sour cream

Heat 2 tablespoons oil in a large skillet over medium heat. Add hashbrowns and red pepper. With a spatula, spread in an even layer; press down lightly. Cook for 6 to 7 minutes, until golden on bottom. Drizzle with remaining oil; turn hashbrowns over in sections. Continue to cook until tender and golden. Remove hashbrowns to a plate; cover to keep warm. Add butter to same skillet; melt butter over medium-low heat. Add eggs; cook for 3 to 4 minutes, stirring occasionally, until set but still moist. Return hashbrowns to skillet; gently mix with eggs. Sprinkle with cilantro and cheese; cook until cheese is melted. Top with salsa and sour cream. Serves 6.

Overnight grits cook up creamy and perfect every time. Following package directions, add the desired amount of long-cooking grits to a slow cooker, plus twice the amount of water specified. Season with salt. Cover and cook on low setting for 7 to 8 hours, stirring in more water toward the end, if needed. Top with butter, shredded cheese or a splash of cream....delicious!

Harvest
for Sharing

Cast-Iron Skillet Loaded Breakfast Biscuits

Courtney Stultz
Weir, KS

These biscuits are full of hearty breakfast ingredients like eggs, bacon, mushrooms and cheese! They're great to cook up and freeze for a quick weekday breakfast option. While I don't use our cast-iron skillet as often as I'd like, it is my favorite way to cook up breakfast. This recipe uses the skillet in a couple different ways.

4 slices bacon
1 c. mushrooms, diced
1/3 c. onion, diced
1 clove garlic, minced
4 eggs, beaten
2 c. all-purpose flour

1 T. baking powder
1 t. sea salt
1/2 c. chilled butter, diced
1 c. buttermilk
1/2 c. shredded Cheddar cheese

In a cast-iron skillet over medium-low heat, cook bacon just until crisp. Drain bacon and set aside, reserving drippings in skillet. Add mushrooms, onion and garlic to skillet; sauté over medium heat until soft. Remove vegetables from pan. Add eggs to skillet and stir to scramble over low heat for 5 to 7 minutes, just until set. Remove from heat. In a large bowl, combine flour, baking powder and salt; cut in butter with a fork. Add buttermilk; mix until just combined. Gently fold in crumbled bacon, vegetables, eggs and cheese. Gently scoop dough into 2-inch balls; arrange in same skillet. (If skillet isn't oven-safe, use a lightly greased baking pan.) Bake, uncovered, at 400 degrees for about 15 to 20 minutes, until lightly golden and cooked through. Makes 8 servings.

Start a tailgating Saturday right...invite friends to join you for breakfast. Keep it simple with a breakfast casserole, baskets of sweet rolls and a fresh fruit salad. It's all about food and friends!

Cozy Breakfasts
for Sharing

Autumn Oat Bars

Melanie Springer
Canton, OH

These delicious bars are perfect for snacks and even for grab & go breakfasts. Try them and see!

2/3 c. butter
1/2 c. pure maple syrup
1/3 c. brown sugar, packed
1/3 c. chopped walnuts, toasted
1 t. vanilla extract

1/4 t. cinnamon
3 c. quick-cooking oats, uncooked
1 c. all-purpose flour

In a saucepan, combine all ingredients except oats and flour. Cook and stir over medium heat for about 4 minutes, until butter is melted. Add oats and flour; stir well. Press into a well-greased 13"x9" baking pan. Score lightly into 24 bars. Bake at 350 degrees for 20 to 24 minutes, until golden. Cut along scoring. Leftovers can be wrapped and stored at room temperature for up to a week. Makes 2 dozen.

Pumpkin Spice Muffins

Charlotte Smith
Huntingdon, PA

Super easy, yummy and great for a quick brunch!

15-1/4 oz. pkg. spice cake mix
15-oz. can pumpkin
3 eggs, beaten

1/3 c. oil
1/3 c. water

Combine all ingredients in a bowl; beat well. Spoon batter into 24 greased or paper-lined muffin cups, filling 2/3 full. Bake at 350 degrees for 20 minutes, or until golden. Makes 2 dozen.

Cream cheese spread for muffins!
Into an 8-ounce container
of whipped cream cheese, stir
2 tablespoons brown sugar and
2 teaspoons cinnamon. Yummy!

Harvest *for Sharing*

Light & Crispy Waffles

Bessie Branyon
Birmingham, AL

I found this recipe online years ago. These waffles make a good fall breakfast...they are very light and airy. Scrumptious with butter and maple syrup!

1-1/4 c. all-purpose flour
1 c. crispy rice cereal
3/4 c. cornstarch
1/4 c. sugar
1 t. baking powder
1/2 t. baking soda

3/4 t. salt
2 eggs, separated
1-1/2 c. milk
1/2 c. oil
1 t. vanilla extract

In a large bowl, stir together flour, cereal, cornstarch, sugar, baking powder, baking soda and salt; set aside. In another bowl, whisk together egg yolks, milk, oil and vanilla. Add to flour mixture and whisk until combined; set aside. In a separate bowl, beat egg whites with an electric mixer on high speed until soft peaks form. Whisk beaten egg whites into batter until just combined; do not overmix. Preheat a waffle iron to medium. Pour 2/3 cup batter per waffle into center of waffle iron; spread batter with the back of a spoon toward outer edges. Close lid and cook until deeply golden, 3 to 4 minutes. Makes 6 waffles.

Whip up some tasty Hot Cranberry Butter Sauce for pancakes and French toast. In a saucepan, stir together a can of whole-berry cranberry sauce, 1/4 cup brown sugar and 1/4 cup butter. Cook and stir over medium heat until well blended and bubbly.

Cozy Breakfasts
for Sharing

Skillet Apples

Bethi Hendrickson
Danville, PA

*Serve these yummy apples as a topping for pancakes or waffles,
as a dessert or even a snack. Yummy served warm
with whipped cream.*

1/3 c. butter
1/2 c. sugar
2 T. cornstarch
4 tart apples, peeled, cored and
    thickly sliced

1-1/2 c. water
1/2 t. cinnamon
1/4 t. allspice

Melt butter in a skillet over medium heat; stir in sugar and cornstarch.
Add apples to skillet along with water and spices. Cover and cook over
medium heat until apples are tender, stirring occasionally. Makes
4 servings.

Autumn's resting on the hills.
Harvested are fruit and grain,
And the home with gladness thrills.
Buckwheat cakes are back again!

–Edgar A. Guest

Harvest
for Sharing

Breakfast Burritos

Karen Wilson
Defiance, OH

These are great for breakfast or brunch! For a larger crowd, I like to make a double batch and keep them warm in the oven.

1 lb. ground pork sausage
1/2 c. onion, chopped
1/2 c. red or green pepper,
   chopped
4-oz. can sliced mushrooms,
   drained
1 T. butter

6 eggs, beaten
2 T. milk
salt and pepper taste
8 10-inch flour tortillas
1 c. shredded Cheddar cheese
Optional: salsa

Brown sausage in a skillet over medium heat. Remove sausage from skillet and drain, reserving 2 tablespoons drippings in skillet. Add onion, pepper and mushrooms to skillet; sauté until tender. Return sausage to skillet; stir into vegetable mixture. Meanwhile, melt butter in another skillet over medium heat. Whisk together eggs and milk; add to skillet. Cook, stirring gently, until eggs are set; season with salt and pepper. Onto each tortilla, spoon equal amounts of sausage mixture, scrambled eggs and cheese. Fold up sides of tortilla over filling and roll up, burrito-style. Serve with salsa, if desired. Burritos may be kept warm in a 200-degree oven. Makes 8 servings.

On a chilly morning, whip up some special hot cocoa with a round disc of Mexican chocolate...the sugar and cinnamon are already mixed in! Bring 4 cups milk almost to a boil, add the chopped chocolate and whisk until it's melted and creamy.

Cozy Breakfasts
for Sharing

Mini Muffin Doughnuts

Carol Lytle
Columbus, OH

Tender and tasty...bet you can't eat just one!

1 c. sugar, divided
1/2 c. butter, melted and divided
3/4 t. nutmeg
1/2 c. milk

1 c. all-purpose flour
1 t. baking powder
1 t. cinnamon

Mix 1/2 cup sugar, 1/4 cup butter and nutmeg in a large bowl. Stir in milk; mix in flour and baking powder until just combined. Spoon batter into 24 generously greased mini muffin cups, filling 1/2 full. Bake at 375 degrees for 15 to 20 minutes, until lightly golden on top. Meanwhile, add remaining melted butter to a bowl. In a separate bowl, mix together remaining sugar and cinnamon. Remove muffins from cups; dip each muffin into melted butter and roll in cinnamon-sugar. Let cool and serve. Makes 2 dozen.

Spiced Tea with Ginger

Carrie O'Shea
Marina del Rey, CA

Warm and cozy on a chilly morning.

3 c. water
1-1/2 inch piece fresh ginger,
    peeled and halved lengthwise
2 c. whole milk
4 black tea bags

4-inch cinnamon stick
8 whole cloves
1/4 t. whole peppercorns
1/4 c. honey

In a large saucepan over medium heat, bring water to a boil. Add ginger. Reduce to a simmer; cook for 8 minutes. Add milk, tea bags and spices, enclosing spices in a spice bag. Simmer over medium-low heat until fragrant, about 6 minutes. Discard tea bags, ginger and spice bag. Stir in honey and serve. Makes 4 servings.

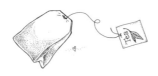

Harvest
for Sharing

Overnight Egg Bake

Bethany Richter
Canby, MN

This is a great recipe to make when you're at the lake cabin or having overnight guests at home. Just toss your ingredients into the slow cooker before you go to bed, and in the morning, your breakfast is ready to serve. Serve with blueberry muffins and hot coffee or tea for a perfect breakfast or brunch.

1 doz. eggs
4 c. milk
10 to 12 slices bread, cubed
2 t. dry mustard

3 c. shredded Cheddar or
   Cheddar Jack cheese
2 c. cooked ham, diced

Beat eggs in a large bowl; whisk in milk. Fold in remaining ingredients; spoon into an ungreased 6-quart slow cooker. Cover and cook on low setting for 7 to 8 hours. Makes 10 to 12 servings.

Apple Cider Doughnuts

Eleanor Dionne
Beverly, MA

These doughnuts are so yummy...easy, too!

2 c. biscuit baking mix
1/2 c. apple cider
3 T. sugar

1 T. cinnamon
oil for deep frying

In a bowl, stir together biscuit mix and cider until a soft dough forms. In a shallow bowl, combine sugar and cinnamon; set aside. Roll out dough on a floured surface, 1/2-inch thick. Cut out doughnuts and centers, using 2-1/2 inch and one-inch cutters; reshape dough scraps as needed. In a large heavy saucepan, heat 2 inches of oil until a deep-fry thermometer reads 350 degrees. Working in batches, cook doughnuts and holes until cooked through, turning once, one to 2 minutes. Transfer to paper towels to drain; toss in cinnamon-sugar to coat. Makes about one dozen.

Keep apple pie spice on hand to use in all kinds of
baked goods...even sprinkle it into hot coffee and cider.

Cozy Breakfasts
for Sharing

Stuffed French Toast

Rebecca Wright
Tulsa, OK

*Delicious toast sandwiches filled with jam and cream cheese...yum!
Make this the night before and leave in the fridge overnight, then bake
the next morning...so convenient. Use spreadable plain cream cheese,
if you like.*

8 slices Texas toast bread	2 c. milk
1/2 c. cream cheese, softened	1 T. cinnamon
1/2 c. favorite jam	Optional: maple syrup or
6 eggs, beaten	powdered sugar

Spread 4 slices bread on one side with cream cheese. Arrange
bread cheese-side up in a buttered 13"x9" baking pan; top each with
2 tablespoons jam and spread to the edges. Top each slice with another
slice of bread; set aside. Whisk together eggs and milk in a bowl; pour
over bread, covering all. Sprinkle with cinnamon. Cover with aluminum
foil and refrigerate overnight. The next morning, remove from
refrigerator. Uncover and bake at 350 degrees for about 30 minutes,
until lightly golden. Serve with syrup or sprinkle with powdered sugar,
if desired. Makes 4 servings.

For a sweet autumn decoration, line the mantel with lots of
votives tucked inside orange, gold, brown and green votive
holders. Surround them with apples, acorns and bittersweet vines.

Harvest
for Sharing

Blueberry Bread

*Joan Raven
Cicero, NY*

Our family welcomes Thanksgiving morning with the aroma of fresh-baked blueberry bread. We have had a tradition of starting Thanksgiving Day with a candlelight breakfast for over 40 years. We welcome parents, grandparents, children, grandchildren and sometimes college friends from years past, gathered at our breakfast table. This bread is a family favorite bursting with blueberries... it's the best!

1 c. fresh blueberries	1 t. vanilla extract
2-1/4 c. all-purpose flour, divided	3 eggs
	1/2 c. milk
2/3 c. butter	1 t. baking powder
1-1/2 c. sugar	1 t. salt

Place blueberries in a bowl; sprinkle with one teaspoon flour and set aside. In a large bowl, stir butter until softened; add sugar and blend well. Add vanilla and eggs, one at a time; add milk and mix well. Add remaining flour, baking powder and salt; mix well. Gently fold in blueberries. Spoon into a greased and floured 9"x5" loaf pan. Bake at 300 degrees for about one hour to 1-1/2 hours, until a toothpick inserted in the center comes out clean. Makes one loaf.

Not too hot, not too cold...autumn is a great time for getting outside. Place a hook by the back door and keep a favorite sweater on it. You never know when you'll want to step outside to see the colorful trees or a bright harvest moon.

Cozy Breakfasts
for Sharing

Baked Eggs & 4 Cheeses

Vickie
Gooseberry Patch

The perfect dish for a brunch buffet! It serves a crowd and is easily made ahead of time and refrigerated. Bake for 60 minutes if chilled.

7 eggs, beaten
1 c. milk
2 t. sugar
16-oz. container small-curd
    cottage cheese
8-oz. pkg. shredded Cheddar
    cheese
8-oz. pkg. shredded Monterey
    Jack cheese

1/2 c. cream cheese, softened
    and cubed
6 T. butter, softened
1/2 t. fresh chives, thyme or dill,
    chopped
1/2 c. all-purpose flour
1 t. baking powder

In a large bowl, whisk together eggs, milk and sugar. Add all cheeses, butter and chives; mix well. Add flour and baking powder; mix again. Spoon into a greased 13"x9" glass baking pan. Bake, uncovered, at 325 degrees for 45 to 50 minutes, until a knife tip inserted in the center comes out clean. Cut into squares. Makes 10 to 12 servings.

The holidays bring lots of brunch occasions with egg dishes
for sharing. Fresh eggs can safely be refrigerated for 4 to 5 weeks,
so go ahead and stock up when they're on sale!

Harvest
for Sharing

Velvet's Weekend Frittata

Velvet Andrews
Cincinnati, OH

An easy and delicious brunch dish to share with family & friends.
Just add a fruit salad and a basket of muffins.

5 slices bacon, diced
1 c. cooked ham, diced
1 onion, diced
6 eggs, beaten
3/4 c. cottage cheese
2 green onions, diced
2 t. dried dill weed

Cajun seasoning to taste
salt and pepper to taste
20-oz. pkg. refrigerated shredded
 hashbrowns
Garnish: tomato slices, shredded
 Cheddar and/or Swiss cheese

Cook bacon in a cast-iron or other oven-proof skillet over medium heat; partially drain. Add ham and onion; sauté until onion is tender. Meanwhile, beat eggs in a large bowl; stir in cottage cheese, green onions and seasonings. Add hashbrowns to bacon mixture in skillet; stir and press down. Remove from heat; add egg mixture to skillet. Bake, uncovered, at 350 degrees for 25 minutes. Top with tomato slices and cheese; broil until lightly golden and cheese is melted. Makes 8 servings.

Egg dishes are a perfect way to use up tasty tidbits from the fridge...cooked ham, crumbled bacon, chopped veggies and cheese. Warm briefly in a skillet and set aside for an omelet filling, or scramble the eggs right in.

Cozy Breakfasts
for Sharing

Heloisa's Oat Muffins

Georgia Muth
Penn Valley, CA

These muffins are perfect as a grab & go breakfast or an after-school snack. My friend Heloisa shared this recipe with me years ago. Blueberries or chocolate chips can be added, if desired.

1 c. quick-cooking oats,
    uncooked
1 c. buttermilk
1 c. all-purpose flour
1-1/4 t. baking powder
1/2 t. baking soda

1 t. salt
3/4 t. cinnamon
1 egg, lightly beaten
1/2 c. brown sugar, packed
1/3 c. oil
Optional: 3/4 c. chopped nuts

In a small bowl, stir together oats and buttermilk; set aside. In a large bowl, stir together flour, baking powder, baking soda, salt and cinnamon. Add egg to oat mixture and beat well; stir in brown sugar. Add flour mixture and oil; stir until moistened. Scoop batter into 12 greased muffin cups, filling about 2/3 full. Sprinkle with chopped nuts, if desired. Bake at 400 degrees for 16 to 20 minutes, until a toothpick inserted in the center comes out clean. Makes one dozen.

A baker's secret! Grease muffin cups on the bottoms and just halfway up the sides...the muffins will bake up nicely puffed on top.

Harvest
for Sharing

Banana-Nut Baked Oatmeal

Kristin Pittis
Dennison, OH

This is a delicious and filling breakfast. It's also great for meal prepping because it keeps well in the refrigerator. Just portion it out and reheat when you're ready to eat!

1/2 c. all-purpose flour
1/3 c. sugar
1/3 c. brown sugar, packed
1/4 c. oil
2 eggs, beaten
2 t. baking powder
1 t. salt

1/4 t. cinnamon
1 c. milk
1 ripe banana, mashed
1/2 c. chopped walnuts or pecans
3 c. old-fashioned oats,
   uncooked

In a large bowl, mix flour, sugars, oil and eggs until smooth. Add baking powder, salt, cinnamon, milk and banana; mix well. Fold in nuts and oats. Spoon into a greased 13"x9" baking pan. Bake, uncovered, at 350 degrees for 30 minutes. Cut into squares to serve. Makes 10 servings.

The first day back to school usually means a busy morning, so why not make a simple overnight breakfast dish? Putting it together the night before means less fuss in the morning, and the kids get off to a great start.

Cozy Breakfasts
for Sharing

French Toast Strata Pie

JoAnn
Gooseberry Patch

Our friends can count on us to make this delicious pie for breakfast when they visit overnight. I love it because it's a great make-ahead!

1/2 lb. ground country-style
   pork sausage
1 tart apple, peeled, cored and
   thinly sliced
5 eggs
2 c. milk

1/3 c. pure maple syrup
1/2 t. nutmeg
1/2 loaf French bread, sliced
   1/2-inch thick and divided
Garnish: additional maple syrup

Brown and crumble sausage in a skillet over medium heat; drain. Remove sausage from skillet; set aside. Add apple slices to skillet; cover and cook for 3 minutes. Beat eggs in a bowl; whisk in milk, maple syrup and nutmeg. Arrange 3/4 of the bread slices in a buttered 10" pie plate. Top with sausage and apples; arrange remaining bread on top. Pour milk mixture evenly over top. Cover and refrigerate overnight. Bake, uncovered, at 350 degrees for 55 to 60 minutes, until set and golden. Cut into wedges; serve with additional syrup. Makes 6 to 8 servings.

Take your family's breakfast outdoors! Spread a quilt on the picnic table and enjoy the cool morning air.

Harvest
for Sharing

Brown Sugar Baked Oatmeal

Karen Wald
Dalton, OH

This oatmeal is delicious topped with sliced ripe peaches,
blueberries and a splash of milk. I use this recipe often!

1 egg, beaten
1/3 c. canola oil
1/3 c. brown sugar, packed
1 c. long-cooking oats,
   uncooked

1 c. quick-cooking oats,
   uncooked
1-1/2 t. baking powder
1/4 t. salt
3/4 c. oat milk or dairy milk

Combine egg, oil and brown sugar in a bowl; whisk well. Add remaining ingredients and mix all together. Spread into a greased 9"x9" glass baking pan. Bake at 350 degrees for 25 minutes. Cut into squares; serve warm or at room temperature. Makes 9 servings.

Fall memories are sharing the season with
All my family & friends around a huge bonfire
Watching the leaves fall
Drinking hot chocolate and hot apple cider
Sharing memories of years gone by
Laughing and sometimes crying
Just enjoying loved ones.
I am ready for a crisp fall day!
And maybe a piece of pumpkin pie.

–Judy Lange, Imperial, PA

Cozy Breakfasts *for Sharing*

Puffy Pancake with Fruit

Shirley Condy
Plainview, NY

This recipe is always a hit at breakfast...guests love it!

2/3 c. water
1/4 c. butter, sliced
1 c. biscuit baking mix

4 eggs
21-oz. can fruit pie filling

Bring water to a boil in a large saucepan over medium heat. Add butter and biscuit mix; cook and stir over low heat for one minute. Remove from heat. Add eggs, one at a time, beating until smooth and glossy. Pour batter into a greased 13"x9" baking pan. Bake at 400 degrees for 30 to 35 minutes, until puffed and dry. Warm pie filling, if desired; spread pie filling over pancake. Cut into squares; serve immediately. Makes 8 to 10 servings.

Quick & Easy Cinnamon Buns

Judy Lange
Imperial, PA

A yummy breakfast that's simple to make and fun to share.

20 frozen yeast dough rolls
1 c. brown sugar, packed
1/4 c. instant vanilla
    pudding mix

3/4 c. raisins
2 T. cinnamon
1/2 c. butter, melted

Layer frozen rolls in a greased 10" Bundt® pan. Sprinkle rolls with brown sugar, dry pudding mix, raisins and cinnamon; drizzle with melted butter. Cover with a tea towel; let rise for 4 hours, or until doubled. Uncover; bake at 350 degrees for 25 minutes. Turn out buns onto a plate and serve. Makes 20 rolls.

Mix pancake or waffle batter in
a wide-mouth, spouted pitcher,
then pour right onto the griddle...
fewer dishes to wash!

Apple Pie Monkey Bread

Audra Vanhorn
Roper, NC

Your taste buds will do back-flips while eating this...
it's insanely good! Yummy!

21-oz. can apple pie filling
1/4 c. brown sugar, packed
1/4 c. sugar
1 T. all-purpose flour
1/2 t. cinnamon
1/4 t. nutmeg

1/4 t. salt
2 T. butter, melted
2 16.3-oz. tubes refrigerated
jumbo flaky biscuits, cut
into quarters

Add pie filling to a large bowl; cut apple slices into bite-size pieces with a knife. Add remaining ingredients except biscuits; mix well. Add biscuit quarters; mix gently to coat well. Add mixture to a well-greased Bundt® pan. Bake at 350 degrees for 45 minutes. Turn out onto a cake plate; drizzle with Glaze and serve. Serves 10.

Glaze:

1 c. powdered sugar
1/4 t. cinnamon

1/4 t. vanilla extract
1 to 2 T. milk

Mix together all ingredients, adding milk to desired consistency.

Happiness is a reward that comes to those that
have not looked for it.
–Emile Chartier

Cozy Breakfasts
for Sharing

Apple Butter Bread

Narita Roady
Pryor, OK

This bread is delicious toasted...a sweet addition to bacon and eggs for breakfast! It's nice to make for special occasions.

2 c. all-purpose flour
1 T. baking soda
1 t. salt
1/4 c. sugar
1-1/2 t. cinnamon
2 eggs

3/4 c. apple butter
1/4 c. margarine, melted
2 T. apple juice
1/2 c. chopped pecans or walnuts
1/2 c. raisins

Combine flour, baking soda, salt, sugar and cinnamon in a bowl; mix well and set aside. Beat eggs in another bowl; stir in apple butter, melted margarine and apple juice. Add flour mixture to egg mixture; stir well. Fold in nuts and raisins. Spoon batter into a greased 9"x5" loaf pan. Bake at 350 degrees for 55 minutes. Cool in pan for 15 minutes; turn loaf out of pan and slice. Makes one loaf.

Many farmers' markets are open well into autumn. Visit a nearby market for just-harvested fruits & vegetables, eggs, baked goods, jams & jellies...perfect for farm-fresh breakfasts.

Harvest
for Sharing

Game-Day Breakfast Casserole

Rhonda Reeder
Ellicott City, MD

*Friends will cheer when you bring this tasty casserole to your
next tailgating brunch! It's an easy make-ahead,
since it's put together the night before.*

1 lb. ground pork breakfast
    sausage, browned and
    drained
2 c. plain croutons
1/4 c. canned diced green chiles
1/4 c. sliced mushrooms

8-oz. pkg. shredded Cheddar
    Jack cheese
8 eggs, beaten
2 c. milk
1 t. dry mustard
1/4 t. salt

In a large bowl, combine browned sausage, croutons, chiles, mushrooms
and cheese. Mix well; spoon into a greased 13"x9" baking pan and set
aside. In another bowl, whisk together eggs, milk, mustard and salt;
pour over sausage mixture in pan. Cover and refrigerate at least
12 hours. One hour before serving time, uncover. Bake at 325 degrees
for one hour. Serves 8 to 10.

Easy Coffee Punch

Dana Cunningham
Lafayette, LA

Perfect for sipping on unseasonably warm fall days.

6 c. whole milk
1 c. chocolate syrup
6 c. brewed coffee, cooled

5 scoops coffee ice cream
5 scoops vanilla ice cream

Mix together milk and chocolate syrup in a large pitcher; stir in
coffee. Cover and refrigerate until chilled. To serve, pour into a large
punchbowl; add ice cream to punchbowl. Ladle punch into cups and
serve. Makes 15 to 18 servings.

Cozy Breakfasts
for Sharing

Yogurt Biscuits

Constance Bockstoce
Dallas, GA

I love to use this recipe for tasty breakfast sandwiches.
These biscuits hold up better than most biscuit recipes.

2 c. all-purpose flour
1 T. baking powder
3/4 t. baking soda
3/4 t. salt
3/4 c. plain Greek yogurt

1/4 to 1/2 c. cold milk
1 t. vinegar
1 egg, beaten
1 T. butter, melted

In a bowl, whisk together flour, baking powder, baking soda and salt; set aside. In a separate bowl, mix together yogurt, 1/4 cup milk, vinegar and egg. Add yogurt mixture to flour mixture; mix until a dough ball is formed. If too dry, slowly stir in remaining milk, a little at a time. On a floured surface, shape dough into a rectangle, about 1-1/2 inches thick. Cut into 6 to 8 squares with a floured knife. Place on a parchment paper-lined baking sheet, 2 inches apart; brush with melted butter. Bake at 400 degrees for 12 to 15 minutes, until golden. Makes 6 to 8 biscuits.

Potato skins for breakfast...yummy! The day before, bake potatoes until tender. Halve and scoop out pulp to enjoy for supper; refrigerate skins overnight. In the morning, warm potato skins in the microwave. Heap with scrambled eggs, bacon bits and cheese. Sure to be a hit!

Harvest
for Sharing

Verna's Superior Pancakes

Agnes Ward
Ontario, Canada

This is a tried & true recipe my sister gave me.

1 egg, beaten
3 T. butter, softened
3 T. sugar
1 t. vanilla extract
1-1/4 c. milk or ginger ale

1-1/2 c. all-purpose flour
4 t. baking powder
1/2 t. salt
Garnish: butter, maple syrup

In a large bowl, beat egg, butter, sugar and vanilla; add milk or ginger ale and mix well. In another bowl, sift flour, baking powder and salt; add to egg mixture and stir until fairly smooth. Drop batter by tablespoonfuls onto a hot greased skillet or griddle. Cook until golden on the bottom; turn over and cook other side. Serve with butter and maple syrup. Makes 6 pancakes.

Stir up a super-simple fruit topping for pancakes and waffles. Combine a can of fruit pie filling and 2 tablespoons orange or apple juice in a small bowl. Microwave for 2 to 2-1/2 minutes, stirring twice. Serve warm.

Cozy Breakfasts
for Sharing

Pecan Pie Muffins

Brenda Schlosser
Brighton, CO

This recipe is so easy and uses only five ingredients. Everyone who tries these muffins wants more! I would rather have these than pecan pie. Great for breakfast with hot tea or coffee, as a midday snack or for dessert with ice cream. The last time I baked these, I made three batches. Enjoy the best thing you've ever put in your mouth!

1 c. chopped pecans
1 c. brown sugar, packed
1/2 c. all-purpose flour

2 eggs, very well beaten
2/3 c. butter, melted and
   slightly cooled

In a bowl, mix together pecans, brown sugar and flour; set aside. Beat eggs in another bowl; add melted butter and mix well. Add egg mixture to pecan mixture; stir until well mixed. Scoop batter into greased muffin cups, filling 2/3 full. Bake at 350 degrees for about 20 to 25 minutes; do not overbake. Cool completely and turn out of pan. Makes one dozen.

Fill a basket or vintage lunchbox with muffins and deliver to
a busy mom. She'll love the surprise and will have a
sweet & simple after-school treat for the kids.

Italian Ham & Egg Bake

Mary Hughes
Talladega, AL

Great for day-after breakfasts, using leftover holiday ham.
Jazz it up with some roasted red peppers!

1 doz. eggs
15-oz. container ricotta cheese or
   cottage cheese
1/2 c. all-purpose flour
1 t. baking powder

8-oz. pkg. shredded Italian-blend
   cheese
2 c. baked ham, diced
1/4 c. green onions, minced

Beat eggs in a large bowl. Add ricotta or cottage cheese, flour and
baking powder; mix well. Stir in shredded cheese, ham and onions.
Spoon into a greased 13"x9" glass baking pan. Bake, uncovered, at
350 degrees for 40 to 50 minutes, until puffed, golden and a knife tip
inserted near center comes out clean. Let stand 5 minutes; cut into
squares and serve. Makes 10 servings.

Dress up breakfast cups and napkins for a tailgating brunch!
Press leaf and pumpkin stickers on plain paper cups, and use
rubber stamps on paper napkins.

Cozy Breakfasts
for Sharing

Bacon & Egg Breakfast Cupcakes

*Ginny Watson
Scranton, PA*

*Breakfast in a biscuit! We all love these. Dress 'em up
with a sprinkle of shredded cheese.*

1 lb. sliced bacon
16.3-oz. tube refrigerated
    homestyle buttermilk
    biscuits, separated

8 eggs
salt and pepper to taste

In a skillet over medium heat, cook bacon for about 4 minutes, until
cooked but not crisp. Set aside bacon on paper towels to drain.
Meanwhile, spray 8 jumbo muffin cups with non-stick vegetable spray.
Place one biscuit in each muffin cup, pressing dough 3/4 of the way up
the side. Criss-cross 2 bacon slices in each biscuit cup; break an egg into
each cup. Season with salt and pepper. Bake, uncovered, at 350 degrees
for 25 to 30 minutes, until eggs are set to desired doneness. Loosen
cups with a small knife; serve immediately. Serves 8.

Fuss-free favorites like Bacon & Egg Breakfast Cupcakes
are ideal for overnight guests on Thanksgiving morning.
Everyone can easily help themselves while
the day's fun is beginning.

Harvest
for Sharing

Harvest Breakfast Casserole

Nancy Lambert
West Jordan, UT

This recipe uses hashbrowns rather than bread cubes. The hashbrowns give a nice change of pace to the traditional breakfast casserole. I have also used crumbled bacon instead of ham, or both...yummy!

30-oz. pkg. frozen shredded
    hashbrowns, thawed
1 T. butter, melted
8-oz. pkg. shredded Cheddar
    cheese
8-oz. pkg. shredded Swiss cheese

1 c. cooked ham, diced
10 eggs, well beaten
1 c. half-and-half
1/2 c. milk
1/2 t. onion salt
1/2 t. salt

Spread hashbrowns evenly in a 13"x9" baking pan coated with non-stick vegetable spray. Pat into the bottom and up the sides of pan. Drizzle butter evenly over hashbrowns. Bake, uncovered, at 350 degrees for 30 minutes. Remove from oven; sprinkle evenly with cheeses and ham. Beat eggs in a large bowl; whisk in half-and-half, milk and seasonings. Pour over hashbrowns. Return to oven; bake an additional 35 to 40 minutes. Serves 8 to 12.

The smell of burning leaves brings back wonderful memories of childhood to me. We had many maple trees in our yard when I was growing up, and every fall we would rake them into piles and burn them. What fun we had playing in the piles before the burn began. We would get on the swing and go as high as we could, then jump off into the piles of leaves! It was a blast, and amazingly there were no broken bones! Then we would start burning the leaves, and keep raking them together until nothing but ashes was left. Oh, what wonderful memories and smells!

–Pam Hooley, LaGrange, IN

Cozy Breakfasts
for Sharing

Dark Chocolate-Cranberry Granola Bars

Dawn Parker
Madison, WI

I love a little something to enjoy with my tea for breakfast every morning. After buying granola bars for years, I figured I can make them myself and control the sugar amounts too.

2 c. old-fashioned oats, uncooked
1/2 c. slivered or chopped almonds
1/3 c. honey
1/4 c. butter
1/2 t. vanilla extract
1 T. brown sugar, packed
1/2 c. dried cranberries
1/2 of a 1-1/2 oz. dark chocolate candy bar, chopped

Spread oats and almonds evenly on a parchment paper-lined baking sheet. Bake at 350 degrees for 5 minutes; stir and bake another 5 minutes. Remove from oven; transfer to a bowl and set aside. Using the same parchment paper, line an 8"x8" baking pan, extending ends over both sides. Set aside. Combine honey, butter, vanilla and brown sugar in a saucepan. Cook and stir over medium heat until butter is melted and and sugar is dissolved. Add to oat mixture and mix well. Fold in cranberries and chocolate. Spoon mixture into prepared pan; fold excess paper over top and press down firmly. Place in freezer for 30 minutes to 2 hours. Remove from freezer; cut into bars. Makes 8 to 10 bars.

Add a splash of color to breakfast and brunch juices! Freeze strawberry slices or blueberries in ice cube trays. Toss several cubes into glasses of juice right before serving.

Grandma George's Onion Gravy & Biscuits

*Tamara Long
Huntsville, AR*

This was a Depression-era recipe from Cozahome, Arkansas. My husband's mom would make this any time she had leftover biscuits. After we'd been married for several years, she finally taught me how to make it. Now that she's gone, it is even more of a comfort food for us, with great memories. The gravy is also good over steak at dinnertime.

16.3-oz. oz. tube refrigerated
  biscuits
2 T. oil
1 c. onion, chopped

2 to 3 T. all-purpose flour
1/2 c. milk
1/2 to 3/4 c. cold water

Bake biscuits according to package directions. Cut biscuits in half; place in a large bowl and set aside. Heat oil in a deep saucepan over medium heat. Add onion; sauté until clear and golden. Stir in flour. Cook, stirring constantly, until very lightly brown. Stir in milk; add cold water until gravy is desired thickness, to make about 8 cups of gravy. Pour over biscuits in bowl and stir together. Serve hot biscuit mixture on its own or over eggs and/or breakfast meats. Makes 6 to 8 servings.

I have always loved fall and its changing colors. One of my fondest fall memories was our church youth group gathering at one of our neighbor's homes for cider and doughnuts in the garage. Then we'd climb into a wagon full of hay and travel the country roads being pulled by a tractor. We country kids thought we were really living it up back then!

–Marsha Baker, Palm Harbor, FL

Favorite
Sides & Salads

Harvest
for Sharing

Autumn Harvest Pasta Salad

June Schwartz
Warren, MI

This tasty recipe filled with fall favorites is sure to please.
It's a light salad that's full of flavor and easy to make...
a lovely addition to autumn meals.

1-1/2 c. rotini pasta, uncooked
3/4 c. plain or cherry-infused
   dried cranberries
3/4 c. celery, chopped
1 navel orange, sectioned
   and halved

1 McIntosh apple, cored
   and diced
1 Bartlett pear, cored and diced
1/3 c. chopped walnuts
1 t. lemon juice
Garnish: crumbled feta cheese

Cook pasta according to package directions; drain. Rinse with cold water; drain and transfer to a large bowl. Add remaining ingredients except garnish; toss to mix. Drizzle with Dressing and garnish with a sprinkling of cheese. Serves 6 to 8.

Dressing:

1/4 c. sugar
1/4 c. olive oil
2 T. cider vinegar
2 T. white wine vinegar

1-1/2 t. poppy seed
1/8 t. dried, minced onions
1/8 t. coarse pepper
1/8 t. paprika

Whisk together all ingredients well.

Pretty placecards in a jiffy! Use metallic ink to
write guests' names on faux autumn leaves.

Favorite
Sides & Salads

Broccoli & Bacon Salad

Charlotte Thacker
Wadesville, IN

This salad recipe was found on an advertisement from our bank several years ago. It is delicious and easy to prepare. I like to peel the broccoli stalks and chop them too.

1 large bunch broccoli, chopped
4 slices bacon, crisply cooked
   and crumbled
1 egg, hard-boiled, peeled
   and chopped

1/2 c. raisins
2 green onions, sliced
1 c. mayonnaise
1/4 c. sugar
2 T. cider vinegar

Combine broccoli, bacon, egg, raisins and onions in a large bowl; toss to mix and set aside. Stir together remaining ingredients in a small bowl; add to broccoli mixture and mix well. Cover and refrigerate until ready to serve. Makes 6 servings.

For the best of the bounty, head to the pumpkin patch early! Just fill a wheelbarrow with pumpkins, squash and gourds for an oh-so-simple harvest decoration. Add some fun with white Lumina pumpkins or orange-red Cinderella pumpkins.

Harvest
for Sharing

Romaine & Pear Salad

Eileen Bennett
Jenison, MI

A fairly new recipe added to our "family favorites" category. So easy to make, and the dressing recipe can be used for any favorite salad. As an added bonus, it's a beautiful salad, perfect for dinner parties! I like to serve this salad in a clear glass bowl.

9-oz. pkg. romaine lettuce leaves
6-oz. pkg. baby spinach

2 Bartlett pears, cored and
   thinly sliced

Prepare Dressing a day ahead; prepare Toasted Pecans ahead. Shortly before serving time, toss together romaine, spinach, pears and toasted pecans in a large bowl. Serve with dressing. Makes 8 to 10 servings.

Dressing:

1/2 c. sour cream
1/2 c. buttermilk
1/4 c. grated Parmesan cheese
1 clove garlic, minced

1/2 t. kosher salt
1 t. coarse pepper
1 t. sugar

Whisk together all ingredients. Cover and refrigerate overnight before serving.

Toasted Pecans:

3/4 to 1 c. chopped pecans

Spread pecans in a single layer on a shallow baking sheet. Bake at 350 degrees for 5 to 6 minutes, stirring once or twice, until lightly browned and fragrant. Let cool.

Favorite
Sides & Salads

Crisp & Easy Apple Salad

Georgia Muth
Penn Valley, CA

I like to use apples from our Fuji, Gala or Pink Lady trees to make this salad. If my apples aren't ripe, apples from the store are fine. You can use one or two varieties of apples together.

1/2 c. pecan halves
4 to 5 apples, cored and cut into
  bite-size cubes
3/4 c. celery, diced
1 c. poppy seed salad dressing

Spread pecans evenly on a baking sheet. Bake at 350 degrees for 10 minutes, until toasted; cool and chop. In a bowl, mix together apples, celery and pecans. Toss with salad dressing; serve immediately. Makes 6 to 8 servings.

Honey-Mustard Coleslaw with Apples

Carolyn Deckard
Bedford, IN

This is one of the great sides we enjoy alongside barbecue sandwiches at our camping get-togethers. It's very easy to make.

16-oz. pkg. shredded
  coleslaw mix
2 apples, cored and cut into
  thin matchsticks
1/2 c. green onions, chopped
1 c. light honey mustard salad
  dressing

Toss together all ingredients in a large bowl. Serve immediately, or cover and refrigerate up to 24 hours. Makes 10 to 12 servings.

Every leaf speaks bliss to me, fluttering from the autumn tree.

–Emily Bronte

Green Chile Corn Soufflé

Judy Borecky
Escondido, CA

I have been making a green chile corn casserole for years, ever since I first received the recipe in 1967. I recently added something to this recipe that turns it into an elegant corn soufflé. I had some leftover corn on the cob, cut it off and added it to the recipe. Delish!

2 eggs, beaten
1/4 c. butter, melted and cooled
   slightly
1 c. light sour cream
1/2 c. cornmeal
15-oz. can creamed corn

3 ears sweet corn, kernels cut off,
   or 2 c. frozen corn, thawed
1 c. shredded Cheddar cheese
4-oz. can diced green chiles
1/2 t. seasoning salt
1/2 t. garlic powder

In a large bowl, whisk together eggs, melted butter, sour cream, cornmeal and all corn. Add remaining ingredients and mix well. Spoon into a lightly greased 2-quart glass casserole dish, 3 inches deep. Bake, uncovered, at 350 degrees for one hour. Serves 6.

Mid-October, here we come! We have fun every Halloween making Jack-o'-Lanterns. Years ago, we started taking our kids on a special yearly trek to our favorite pumpkin farm to choose our favorite pumpkins, apples and of course apple cider. Then we began including their friends, and continue today with added spouses, grandkids and great-grandkids. Back home, pumpkins are lined up on the porch and each person may pick their choice to carve. We always love to have extra pumpkins for those who have never done a Jack-o'-Lantern. Afterwards, on Halloween, with a candle glowing in each, what a wonderful glow all these lanterns make. Great family fun...a great family tradition!

–Sandy Coffey, Cincinnati, OH

Favorite
Sides & Salads

Baked Acorn Squash with Cinnamon Apples

Marsha Baker
Palm Harbor, FL

I could eat nothing but this scrumptious dish and be happy! It's a wonderful fall side that you'll want to serve again & again. Instead of cinnamon and allspice, 1-1/4 teaspoons pumpkin pie spice can be substituted.

2 to 3 acorn squash, halved
    and seeds removed
2 to 3 tart apples, cored and
    chopped
1/3 c. light brown sugar, packed
1/4 c. butter, melted

1 T. all-purpose flour
3/4 t. salt
1 t. cinnamon
1/4 t. ground allspice
1/2 to 3/4 c. water

Arrange squash halves in an ungreased 13"x9" baking pan, cut-side up. Divide apples among squash halves and set aside. In a small bowl, stir together remaining ingredients except water; drizzle over squash. Pour water into pan around squash. Cover pan tightly with aluminum foil. Bake at 350 degrees for about 60 to 70 minutes, until squash is fork-tender. Serves 4 to 6.

The leaves had a wonderful frolic,
They danced to the wind's loud song.
They whirled, and they floated and scampered,
They circled and flew along.

–Anonymous

Cheesy Oniony Hashbrown Casserole

Karen Antonides
Gahanna, OH

This is my son's favorite potato dish. Whenever he comes over for dinner, he always asks, "Are we having the cheesy hashbrowns?" It's an awesome dish for company and the addition of cream of onion soup gives a different spin to an old favorite side dish.

10-3/4 oz. can cream of
    onion soup
8-oz. container sour cream
1/2 c. butter, melted
1 t. salt
1/2 t. pepper
3 c. shredded sharp Cheddar
    cheese, divided

Optional: 1/2 c. crisply cooked,
    crumbled bacon; 1/2 c. sliced
    green onions
30-oz. pkg. frozen shredded
    hashbrowns, thawed

In a large bowl, mix together onion soup, sour cream and melted butter. Season with salt and pepper; blend well. Stir in 2 cups cheese; add crumbled bacon and/or onions, if using. Add hashbrowns and stir together very well. Spread potato mixture evenly in a greased 13"x9" baking pan; top with remaining cheese. Bake, uncovered, at 350 degrees for 45 minutes to one hour, until heated through and golden. Makes 12 to 15 servings.

Thanksgiving is perfect for potlucks! Everyone brings what they're famous for making or just their favorite dish. It's all about celebrating food, family & friends.

3-Cheese Macaroni & Cheese

Rebecca Etling
Blairsville, PA

*This is the ultimate comfort food! It's extra cheesy and creamy.
Smoked Gouda cheese adds an extra taste that we love.*

16-oz. pkg. elbow macaroni,
  uncooked
1/2 c. butter, sliced
1/3 c. all-purpose flour
1-1/2 c. 2% milk
1 c. half-and-half

1 lb. Jack & Jill or Colby Jack
  cheese, cubed
1/2 lb. smoked Gouda cheese,
  cubed
1/2 lb. Longhorn cheese, cubed

Cook macaroni according to package directions, just until tender; drain
and transfer to a greased 13"x9" baking pan. Meanwhile, melt butter in
a large saucepan over medium heat. Add flour, stirring constantly until
thickened; boil gently for one minute. Gradually add milk and half-and-
half, whisking until blended and thickened. Add all cheeses; cook and
stir until melted. Spoon cheese mixture over cooked macaroni; stir
gently until blended. Cover with aluminum foil. Bake at 350 degrees
for 30 minutes, or until edges are bubbly. Remove foil; bake another
10 to 15 minutes, until lightly golden. Let stand at room temperature
for 10 minutes before serving. Makes 8 to 12 servings.

Slip a dress and apron on your scarecrow this season
and she'll be an instant hit as a scarecrone!

Harvest
for Sharing

Grandma Joan's Taco Salad

Nichole Hawkins
Decatur, IN

This is my husband's Grandma Joan's recipe and I now get to make it for everyone. People love the taste of nacho chips and Western dressing with this salad...it's a great flavor and I get many requests for this recipe. All credit goes to Grandma Jo!

1 lb. ground beef
1-1/4 oz. pkg. taco seasoning
   mix
1 head iceberg lettuce, shredded
8-oz. pkg. shredded Cheddar
   cheese
9-oz. pkg. nacho cheese tortilla
   chips, crushed

3 to 4 tomatoes, cubed
2 to 3 green onions, sliced
Optional: 16-oz. can pinto beans,
   drained and rinsed
26-oz. bottle Western salad
   dressing

Brown beef in a skillet over medium heat; drain and stir in taco seasoning. Set aside to cool. Arrange lettuce in a large bowl; layer with shredded cheese, crushed chips, tomatoes, onions and beans, if using. Add browned beef and salad dressing; stir until mixed. Serve immediately to prevent sogginess. Makes 12 to 15 servings.

Host a fun-filled pumpkin carving party this year! Guests can bring their own pumpkins and tools, while you set out water-based paints, glue sticks, glitter and stickers for the kids. Sure to be fun for all!

Favorite
Sides & Salads

Vicki's Linguine & Veggie Salad

Janis Purnell
Littlestown, PA

My sister Vicki used to prepare a pasta salad for family events. When asked for a recipe, she would always say she just tossed some things together. When she passed away, the one thing I wanted to be able to do for family gatherings was to recreate this favorite, especially for her children. I think I have come pretty close to the original, and I think of Vicki every time I prepare it.

16-oz. pkg. linguine pasta,
    uncooked
16-oz. bottle Italian salad
    dressing
2 T. grated Romano cheese
1 t. paprika

3/4 t. celery seed
1/4 t. garlic powder
3/4 t. salt
1/4 t. coarse pepper
1 English cucumber, chopped
1 tomato, chopped

Cook pasta according to package directions; drain well. Rinse with cold water; drain and set aside. In a large bowl, mix together Italian dressing, cheese and seasonings. Add cucumber and tomato to dressing mixture; stir to coat well. Add cooked pasta; toss to mix well. Cover and chill at least 4 hours before serving. Serves 8 to 10.

Give favorite pasta recipes a twist for fall...pick up some pasta
in seasonal shapes like autumn leaves, pumpkins or turkeys!
Some even come in veggie colors like orange, red or green.

Harvest
for Sharing

Apple Chestnut Stuffing

Bethi Hendrickson
Danville, PA

This stuffing is always the favorite at our Thanksgiving table. The chestnuts come from trees my grandfather and father planted years ago on our farm. Although they are both gone now, we enjoy a little gift from them with us every Thanksgiving.

1 c. raw chestnuts	1-1/2 t. poultry seasoning
1/2 c. butter	1/8 t. nutmeg
2 apples, peeled and finely diced	4 to 5 c. bread cubes
1/2 c. onion, finely diced	1 c. milk, warmed
3 stalks celery, finely diced	Optional: 1 c. chicken broth

Score chestnuts with a knife. Place in a saucepan; cover with water. Bring to a boil over medium-high heat. Cook for 5 to 10 minutes, until chestnuts are softened. Drain and cool. Use knife to peel skins from chestnuts; set aside. Meanwhile, melt butter in a large skillet over medium heat. Add apples, onion, celery, chopped chestnuts and seasonings. Simmer over low heat until onion and celery are translucent. Transfer mixture to a large bowl; add bread cubes. Mix together; slowly stir in warm milk. If more liquid is desired, stir in chicken broth as desired. Transfer to a greased 3-quart casserole dish. Cover with aluminum foil and refrigerate for at least 12 hours. Bake at 350 degrees for 45 to 50 minutes or until puffy on top. Uncover; bake another 10 minutes, or until crunchy and lightly golden on top. Makes 8 to 10 servings.

Roll silverware in dinner napkins, then wrap with bittersweet vines or slip on a small grapevine wreath. A simple yet pretty way to bring autumn to the table.

Favorite
Sides & Salads

Stuffed Artichoke Casserole

Annette Ceravolo
Hoover, AL

For your Thanksgiving buffet, a tasty side that's a little different.

3/4 c. onion, chopped
1/3 c. olive oil
2 14-oz. cans artichoke hearts,
    drained and coarsely chopped
3/4 c. Italian-seasoned dry
    bread crumbs

1/2 c. grated Parmesan cheese
1 T. dried parsley
1/2 t. garlic powder

In a small skillet over medium heat, sauté onion in olive oil; drain.
Transfer onion to a large bowl; add remaining ingredients and mix
well. Spoon mixture into a greased 1-1/2 quart casserole dish. Bake,
uncovered, at 350 degrees for 30 minutes, until hot and bubbly. Makes
4 to 5 servings.

Thanksgiving brings back so many wonderful memories of my
mother cooking in her small kitchen. The delightful scents of
cinnamon and nutmeg filled the air as pies baked in the oven and
cooled on the stove. What a treat it was to have a slice of that
homemade pecan or sweet potato pie! Those beloved memories
linger as I prepare my own Thanksgiving meal to share with family
& friends each year. Baking pies and making savory cornbread
dressing from my mother's tried & true recipes makes Thanksgiving
so special for me and others too. Thanksgiving is indeed
the most wonderful time of the year!

–Melody Lenard, Grayson, LA

Harvest
for Sharing

Luscious Onion Casserole

Janis Parr
Ontario, Canada

This is an absolutely scrumptious dish! It may be assembled the day before needed, covered and refrigerated and baked the next day. Sometimes I add some crisp, crumbled bacon for a special touch.

2 c. white onions, sliced
1-1/2 c. sliced mushrooms
7 T. butter, softened and divided
12 slices French bread
1-1/2 c. shredded Swiss cheese
10-3/4 oz. can cream of
    chicken soup

1/2 c. plus 2 T. milk
1 egg, beaten
2 t. soy sauce
salt and pepper to taste

In a skillet over medium heat, sauté onions and mushrooms in 3 tablespoons butter until lightly golden; remove from heat. Spread remaining butter over both sides of bread slices; arrange 6 slices in a greased 13"x9" baking pan. Spoon onion mixture evenly over bread; top with shredded cheese. Arrange remaining bread over cheese. In a small bowl, stir together remaining ingredients; stir well and spoon evenly over bread. Bake, uncovered, at 350 degrees for 35 to 40 minutes. Serves 8 to 10.

Not cool enough for a fire? Give your fireplace a welcoming autumn glow...fill it with pots of flame-colored orange and yellow mums.

Favorite
Sides & Salads

German Green Beans

Judy Borecky
Escondido, CA

My husband's grandmother was German. After she came to America, she spoke German only when she prayed. This easy, tasty recipe reminds me of her.

3 14-1/2 oz. cans cut green
    beans, drained and rinsed
1/2 c. onion, diced
1/3 c. brown sugar, packed

1 c. water
1/3 c. rice vinegar
salt and pepper to taste

Combine all ingredients in a saucepan. Simmer over medium-low heat for 45 minutes, stirring occasionally. Makes 8 servings.

Parmesan Baked Potatoes

Sandy Ward
Anderson, IN

Some of the most memorable meals are made with great ease. This is a simple, delicious side to serve with baked chicken, meatloaf and burgers. It's a family favorite.

6 T. butter, melted
3 T. grated Parmesan cheese

8 redskin potatoes, halved
    lengthwise

Spread melted butter in a 13"x9 baking pan; sprinkle cheese over butter. Arrange potatoes in pan, cut-side down. Bake, uncovered, at 400 degrees for 40 to 45 minutes, until fork-tender. Serves 4 to 6.

A delicious drizzle for steamed veggies! Boil 1/2 cup balsamic vinegar, stirring often, until thickened. So simple and scrumptious.

Harvest
for Sharing

Easy Vegetable Salad

Jahaira Cormier
Westampton, NJ

I love making this marinated salad for barbecues and picnics. It's light and refreshing. I like making it ahead of time and leaving in the refrigerator for a few hours...it just gets better and better!

1 pt. cherry tomatoes, halved
6-oz. can black olives, drained
   and halved
2 cucumbers, peeled, quartered
   and sliced

1/2 red onion, thinly sliced
8-oz. pkg. mozzarella cheese,
   cubed
Italian salad dressing to taste

In a large bowl, combine all ingredients except salad dressing. Add salad dressing to taste; toss gently to mix. Cover and refrigerate; the longer the salad is refrigerated, the better the flavor is. Serves 6.

Serve up a salad topped with grilled apple slices...yummy with pears too! Heat a tablespoon each of olive oil and maple syrup in a skillet. Add thin slices of tart apple. Cook for 6 to 8 minutes, turning once, until deep golden and crisp. Serve warm.

Favorite
Sides & Salads

Favorite Broccoli Salad

Debbie McMurry
Pittsburgh, KS

*A recipe passed down from my mother...always a hit
at family dinners and parties.*

1 c. mayonnaise-style salad
   dressing
1/2 c. sugar
2 T. red wine vinegar
4 c. broccoli, cut into bite-size
   flowerets

1/2 lb. bacon, crisply cooked
   and crumbled
1 c. shredded Cheddar cheese
1/2 c. red onion, chopped
1/2 c. slivered almonds
1/2 c. raisins

Combine salad dressing, sugar and vinegar in a small bowl; mix well
and set aside. In a large bowl, combine remaining ingredients. Add
dressing mixture and toss well. Cover and refrigerate for 4 hours; stir
and serve. Makes 8 to 10 servings.

Tote tossed salads to harvest get-togethers the no-spill way...
packed in a large plastic zipping bag. When you arrive,
simply pour the salad into a serving bowl.

Harvest
for Sharing

Creamy Cheesy Scalloped Potatoes *Shirley Howie*
Foxboro, MA

*This easy-to-prepare dish is always a favorite on my dinner table.
Sometimes I use different kinds of cheese in place of the Cheddar Jack.
Try Swiss cheese for a milder version, or Pepper Jack cheese for more
of a nip!*

1 c. whipping cream
1 c. whole milk
1/2 t. garlic powder
1/2 t. dried thyme
1 t. salt
1/2 t. pepper

2-1/2 lbs. russet potatoes,
   peeled, thinly sliced and
   divided
8-oz. pkg. shredded Cheddar Jack
   cheese, divided
3 T. fresh chives, chopped

In a saucepan over medium heat, stir together cream, milk and
seasonings; bring just to a boil. Remove from heat and set aside. Spread
half of sliced potatoes in a greased 13"x9" baking pan. Spoon half of
sauce evenly over potatoes; sprinkle with half of the cheese. Repeat
layering; top with chives. Cover tightly with aluminum foil. Bake at
425 degrees for 45 minutes. Remove foil and bake for about 10 minutes
more, until golden on top. Allow to rest for 10 minutes before serving.
Makes 6 servings.

For a quick & easy table runner, choose cotton fabric
printed with autumn leaves, Indian corn and pumpkins
in glowing gold, orange and brown. Simply pink the edges...
it will dress up the dinner table all season long!

Favorite
Sides & Salads

Joyce's Squash Casserole

Sandra Turner
Fayetteville, NC

My friend Joyce would bring this to our church Thanksgiving potluck every year and it was always one of my favorite side dishes. After Joyce passed away, I found her recipe and started making it for my family. It is so delicious, I had to share it with others.

3 c. yellow squash, diced
3 c. zucchini, diced
1/2 c. onion, diced
10-3/4 oz. can cream of
   chicken soup
8-oz. container sour cream

1 c. carrots, peeled and grated
8-oz. pkg. shredded Cheddar
   cheese
6-oz. pkg. chicken-flavored
   stuffing mix
1/2 c. butter, melted

Bring a large saucepan of water to a boil over high heat. Add squash, zucchini and onion; cook until fork-tender. Drain well. In a large bowl, stir together chicken soup, sour cream and carrots. Add squash mixture and cheese; stir well. In a separate bowl, toss together stuffing mix and melted butter. Spoon half of stuffing mixture into a greased 13"x9" baking pan; spoon squash mixture over stuffing. Top with remaining stuffing. Bake, uncovered, at 350 degrees for 30 minutes, until heated through and cheese is melted. Makes 8 to 10 servings.

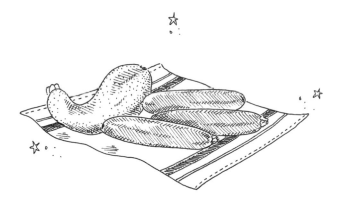

Packing for a potluck or a tailgating party? Safety first! Keep hot foods hot, cold foods cold, and don't let any food sit out longer than 2 hours, even if the food looks just fine.

Butternut Squash Jumble

Kara Brocious
Indianapolis, IN

I took this dish to a Thanksgiving potluck one year when I couldn't go home for the holiday, and it was a huge hit. It's simple to prepare, different without being too non-traditional, and it's even good at room temperature, which helps when you're trying to figure out cooking times for a big dinner. I like Gorgonzola cheese for this, but feta cheese would work too.

2 to 2-1/2 lbs. butternut squash, peeled and cut into 1-inch cubes
2 to 2-1/2 lbs. sweet potatoes, peeled and cut into 1-inch cubes
2 T. olive oil
1 t. dried thyme
2 t. salt
1 t. pepper
1 c. crumbled Gorgonzola cheese
1 c. chopped pecans, toasted
1/2 c. dried cranberries
1/4 c. fresh parsley, chopped

In a large bowl, toss squash and sweet potatoes with oil and seasonings. Spread mixture evenly on a lightly greased 15"x10" jelly-roll pan, or divide between 2 baking sheets. Bake at 425 degrees for 40 to 45 minutes, until tender and a knife tip can be inserted easily. Transfer squash mixture to a serving bowl; add remaining ingredients and toss to mix. Serves 10 to 12.

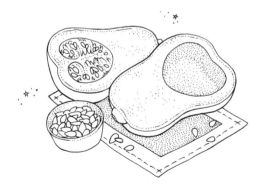

Butternut squash is flavorful and nutritious, but can be difficult to cut. Try this handy tip! Pierce the whole squash all over with a fork and microwave it for 2 to 3 minutes, until softened. The squash will cut easily.

Favorite
Sides & Salads

Grandmother's Molasses Baked Beans

Bethi Hendrickson
Danville, PA

We found this tried & true recipe in my grandmother's recipe box after her passing...and a family favorite continues on.

2 15-1/2 oz. cans Great Northern
   beans, drained
5 slices bacon, diced
3/4 c. brown sugar, packed

1/2 c. catsup
3 T. molasses
1 T. mustard
1/4 t. paprika

Combine all ingredients in a lightly greased 2-quart casserole dish or bean pot; mix well. Bake, uncovered, at 325 degrees for 2-1/2 hours, stirring every 30 minutes. Let stand for 5 to 10 minutes before serving. Serves 8 to 10.

Cranberry Baked Beans

Debra Johnson
Myrtle Beach, SC

Sure to be welcome at any tailgating party or picnic.

3 15-oz. cans pork & beans,
   partially drained
14-oz. can whole-berry
   cranberry sauce
6 slices bacon, diced, partially
   cooked and drained

1 onion, chopped
1/2 c. brown sugar, packed
1/2 c. maple syrup
1/3 c. catsup
2 T. mustard
1 T. Worcestershire sauce

In a large bowl, combine pork & beans, cranberry sauce, bacon and onion; stir well and set aside. In a small bowl, combine remaining ingredients; mix well and stir into bean mixture. Transfer to a greased 3-quart casserole dish. Bake, uncovered, at 350 degrees for 2 hours, or until hot and bubbly. Makes 10 to 12 servings.

Harvest
for Sharing

Cranberry Waldorf Gelatin Salad

Barbara Klein
Newburgh, IN

A tangy, crunchy gelatin salad that's perfect for autumn.

1 env. unflavored gelatin
1 c. cold water, divided
3-oz. pkg. cranberry gelatin mix
2 c. boiling water
14-oz. can whole-berry
   cranberry sauce

1/2 to 1 t. cinnamon
Optional: 1/4 t. ground ginger
1/8 to 1/4 t. salt
2 tart apples, peeled, cored
   and diced
1 c. chopped walnuts

In a large bowl, sprinkle unflavored gelatin over 1/4 cup cold water. Let stand for 5 minutes. Add cranberry gelatin mix and boiling water to softened gelatin; stir until dissolved. Stir in cranberry sauce until well blended. Add spices, salt and remaining cold water. Cover and refrigerate until almost set. Fold in apples and walnuts; transfer to an ungreased 2-1/2 quart serving bowl. Cover and refrigerate until firm. Makes 12 servings.

Making a special holiday gelatin salad in a mold? Loosen it
from the mold in a snap. Dip the bottom of the mold
into warm water. Set a plate over the top of the mold
and turn right-side up...the salad should slip out easily!

Creamy Fruit Salad

Carrie Miller
Dry Fork, VA

At family get-togethers, I am always asked to bring along this fruit salad. The creamy sauce goes well with many types of soft fruit, so feel free to change the fruit to suit your own preferences.

8-oz. pkg. cream cheese, softened
1/4 c. sugar
8-oz. container frozen whipped topping, thawed
20-oz. can pineapple tidbits, drained

15-1/4 oz. can sliced peaches, drained and chopped
15-oz. can mandarin oranges, drained
1-1/2 c. fresh strawberries, hulled and sliced

In a large bowl, beat cream cheese and sugar with an electric mixer on medium speed until well combined. Using a spatula, gently fold whipped topping into cream cheese mixture until combined. Gently fold in fruit, stirring well to make sure all of the fruit is coated in the sauce. Cover and refrigerate for at least 2 hours before serving. Serves 10 to 12.

When draining canned fruit, freeze the juice in ice cube trays. It's handy for adding a little sweetness to marinades and dressings.

Harvest
for Sharing

Grandma Dee's Dressing

Elisha Nelson
Brookline, MO

*At our house, it wouldn't be Thanksgiving without this
dressing next to the roast turkey on the holiday table!*

2 c. cornbread, crumbled
2 c. white bread, cubed
1 T. olive oil
1/2 c. onion, chopped
1/2 c. celery, chopped
1 t. dried sage

1/2 t. salt, or to taste
1/4 t. pepper
2 eggs, beaten
1/4 c. butter, melted and
　　slightly cooled
2 c. turkey or chicken broth

The night before, spread breads on a baking sheet and set out overnight
to dry out. In the morning, heat oil in a skillet over medium heat. Add
onion and celery; sauté until tender. In a large bowl, combine breads and
seasonings; toss to coat evenly. Add onion mixture, eggs, melted butter
and broth to bread mixture; gently mix together. Spoon into a greased
13"x9" baking pan. Bake, uncovered, at 325 degrees for 30 minutes.
Makes 8 to 10 servings.

Dressing, stuffing or filling...whatever you call it, it's even better
with gravy! Measure 1/4 cup pan drippings from a turkey or
beef roast into a skillet over medium heat. Stir in 1/4 cup flour.
Cook and stir until smooth and bubbly. Add 2 cups skimmed
pan juices or broth; cook and stir until boiling. Boil for about
one minute, to desired thickness. Add salt and pepper to taste.

Favorite
Sides & Salads

Roasted Pears & Sweet Potatoes

Mildred Biggin
Lyons, IL

A delicious way to enjoy these autumn favorites. The onions caramelize to add a sweetness that goes very well with roast turkey.

2 Bartlett pears, cored and
   cut into wedges
2 sweet potatoes, peeled and
   cut into 1/2-inch thick
   half-moons
2 small red onions, cut
   into wedges

3 T. extra-virgin olive oil
3 sprigs fresh thyme, or more
   to taste
1 t. salt
1 t. pepper

On a large rimmed baking sheet, toss pears, sweet potatoes and onions with remaining ingredients. Bake at 425 degrees for 35 to 45 minutes, until tender and golden, stirring occasionally. Makes 4 to 6 servings.

Plan a harvest scavenger hunt for the whole family. Send everyone out with a list of fall finds...a golden oak leaf, a red maple leaf, an acorn, a pumpkin, a scarecrow, a red apple and a hay bale, just to name a few. It's not only lots of fun, it's a great way to get outside and enjoy the fabulous fall weather!

Harvest
for Sharing

Cornbread Zucchini Bake

Marian Forck
Chamois, MO

My neighbor Ev made this for a church function...it was a hit!
I love anything with zucchini and just had to have the recipe.

1/2 c. butter, melted
8-1/2 oz. pkg. corn muffin mix
4 eggs, beaten
3 c. zucchini, grated
2 T. garlic, minced

1/4 c. red, yellow and/or green
    pepper, chopped
Optional: 1/4 c. onion, chopped
8-oz. pkg. shredded Cheddar
    cheese

Spread melted butter in a 13"x9" baking pan; set aside. In a bowl, combine dry corn muffin mix and remaining ingredients; mix together and spoon into pan. Bake, uncovered, at 400 degrees for 25 minutes, or until set and golden. Makes 6 servings.

When shopping the garden store for pumpkins and gourds, you'll find plenty of colorful flowers that like the chilly autumn nights. Fill urns and windowboxes with mums, pansies or decorative cabbages.

Favorite
Sides & Salads

Mom's Zucchini Casserole

Helen McKay
Edmond, OK

I remember Mom making this in the late summer and early fall when I was in high school, when zucchini was plentiful!!

4 c. zucchini, cut into chunks
1 c. canned creamed corn
4-oz. can chopped green chiles

1-1/2 c. shredded Cheddar
   cheese
1/4 c. onion, grated

Add zucchini to a saucepan of boiling salted water. Cook until fork-tender; drain very well. Combine remaining ingredients in a bowl; add zucchini and mix well. Transfer to a greased 3-quart casserole dish. Bake, uncovered, at 350 degrees for 30 minutes, or until hot and bubbly. Makes 8 servings.

Homestyle Mashed Potatoes

Lisa Ann Panzino DiNunzio
Vineland, NJ

A perfect side to any Thanksgiving meal!

5 lbs. baking potatoes, peeled
   and cut into 1-inch cubes
1-1/2 t. sea salt, divided

3/4 c. butter
1/4 t. pepper
1 c. milk

Add potatoes and one teaspoon salt to a heavy saucepan. Cover potatoes with water and bring to a boil. Reduce heat to a simmer and cook until potatoes are fork-tender, 20 to 25 minutes. Drain potatoes in a colander; return to pan. Add butter, remaining salt, pepper and milk to potatoes. With a potato masher or electric mixer on medium speed, mash or beat potatoes to desired consistency. Add more butter, milk, salt and pepper, if desired. Serves 6 to 8.

Simmer potatoes in chicken
broth instead of water
for delicious flavor.

Harvest
for Sharing

Mom's Party Salad

Mary Plut
Hackettstown, NJ

Whenever I saw my mom making this salad in her big glass trifle bowl, I knew company was coming over soon! I think she loved being able to prepare it the night before, so she could focus on other foods for party day. Something about the combination of the ingredients always tastes so fresh. Everyone loves a crunchy salad!

6-oz. pkg. fresh spinach
1/2 t. sugar
salt and pepper to taste
6 eggs, hard-boiled, peeled and
    finely chopped
1/2 lb. deli boiled ham, cut into
    thin strips
1/2 lb. deli sliced sandwich
    ham, diced
1 head iceberg lettuce, torn
    or shredded

10-oz. pkg. frozen peas, thawed
    and well drained
1 red onion, sliced
16-oz. container sour cream
1 c. mayonnaise
8-oz. pkg. shredded Swiss cheese
1/2 lb. bacon, crisply cooked
    and crumbled

In a large glass bowl, toss spinach with sugar; season with salt and pepper. In order listed, layer remaining ingredients over spinach except crumbled bacon. Cover with plastic wrap and refrigerate overnight. Just before serving, sprinkle with bacon. Makes 10 to 15 servings.

Serve toasty baguette chips alongside a favorite salad. Thinly slice
a loaf of French bread. Brush slices with olive oil; place on a
baking sheet and sprinkle with grated Parmesan cheese. Bake at
350 degrees until crisp and golden, about 10 minutes.

Favorite
Sides & Salads

Sauerkraut Slaw

Jane Hrabak
Belle Plaine, IA

This recipe is from my mom's recipe stash, and it's a good one! It reminds me that sauerkraut is a great vegetable, and easily used for cold salads. This salad is so easy and great for potlucks...if you don't have a cooler or ice, don't worry, it'll be fine!

14-1/2 oz. jar sauerkraut, rinsed
    and squeezed dry
7-oz. jar diced pimentos
1 c. celery, chopped
3/4 c. green pepper, coarsely
    chopped

1/2 c. onion, chopped
1/3 c. water
1/4 c. vinegar
1 to 1-1/4 c. sugar
1/4 c. oil
1/2 t. salt

In a large bowl, combine sauerkraut, pimentos with juice, celery, green pepper and onion. Toss to mix and set aside. Combine remaining ingredients in a small bowl; pour over sauerkraut mixture. Mix gently. Cover tightly; refrigerate 2 to 3 days before serving. Slaw will become crisp and will keep at least one week. Makes 10 to 12 servings.

My oldest child started reading when she was 3, before online school began. I worked part-time at home while caring for her and a younger sister, so I thought, let's try homeschooling. We ordered up a huge box of curriculum materials and off we went! Thus began a six-year journey together. We ordered up a fresh new grade or box for each of them every 8 months as they "graduated" through the grades. All books, instructions, homework, labs, everything brand-new! Receiving "a fresh box of homeschool" was like Christmas! Each girl had her own colorful desk, chalk boards, maps...delightful years. We loved our school!

–Lisa Staib, Tumbling Shoals, AR

Harvest
for Sharing

Wild Rice with Orange Juice & Cranberries

Louise Soweski
Woodbridge, NJ

I love wild rice...it's delicious and versatile. One day, I decided to cook it with orange juice instead of water, and I added some sweetened dried cranberries. The flavor was incredible! Delicious wild rice cooked in orange juice gave it a citrus tang, and the cranberries topped it off with a tart/sweet finish. Hope you enjoy my recipe!

1 c. wild rice, uncooked
3 to 4. c. orange juice
salt and pepper to taste
1/4 c. onion, diced
1/4 c. celery, diced

2 T. butter, divided
1/8 t. garlic powder
1/2 c. sweetened dried
   cranberries

Cook wild rice according to package directions, substituting orange juice for the water called for. Season with salt and pepper. While rice is cooking, sauté onion and celery in one tablespoon butter in a small skillet over medium heat until soft. Sprinkle with garlic powder; add to rice and continue cooking. About 10 minutes before rice is done, stir in cranberries. Top with remaining butter and serve. Makes 4 servings.

Shake up a simple apple cider vinaigrette for salads. Combine
2 tablespoons cider vinegar, 6 tablespoons olive oil and
one teaspoon Dijon mustard in a small jar. Twist on the lid
and shake well. Season with salt and pepper and serve.

Favorite
Sides & Salads

Barley Mushroom Casserole

Judith Smith
Bellevue, WA

I received this recipe at a holiday party in the 1990s.
It's tasty and easy to prepare.

5 T. butter
8-oz. pkg. sliced mushrooms
1 c. onion, chopped

1 c. pearled barley, uncooked
2 c. beef broth, divided
salt and pepper to taste

Melt butter in a skillet over medium heat; sauté mushrooms and onion until soft. Add barley; sauté until lightly golden, stirring often. Spoon mixture into a buttered 2-quart casserole dish. Pour one cup broth over barley in casserole; season with salt and pepper as desired. Cover and bake at 350 degrees for 30 minutes. Uncover; stir in remaining broth. Continue baking, uncovered, until liquid is absorbed and barley is tender, about 30 minutes. Serves 6 to 8.

Cranberry-Orange Sauce

Liz Plotnick Snay
Gooseberry Patch

I've only started making fresh cranberry sauce a couple of years ago.
It's a hit every Thanksgiving! I buy cranberries a week or two early
and keep them in the freezer until ready to use.

1/2 c. water
1/2 c. sugar
1/2 c. low-sugar orange juice

12-oz. pkg fresh cranberries
15-oz. can mandarin oranges,
    drained

Combine water and sugar in a large saucepan over medium heat. Cook and stir until sugar is dissolved. Add orange juice; bring to a boil. Add cranberries. Return to a boil over medium heat. Boil for 10 minutes, stirring occasionally and popping cranberries on side of pan with spoon. Remove from stove; stir in oranges. Spoon into a heat-safe serving bowl; cover and refrigerate until chilled. Makes 8 to 10 servings.

Harvest
for Sharing

German Potato Salad

Charlene McCain
Bakersfield, CA

My mother used to make this tasty potato salad often. It was always a big hit at picnics and potlucks, as well as at family dinners.

3 lbs. russet potatoes, peeled
  and halved
1 t. salt
1 c. mayonnaise
1/4 c. mustard
2 t. sweet pickle juice
1 t. lemon juice
1/2 t. onion powder

1/4 c. sweet pickles, chopped
1/4 c. sweet pickle relish
1 stalk celery, chopped
1/2 sweet or red onion, chopped
3 eggs, hard-boiled, peeled
  and chopped
salt and pepper to taste
Garnish: paprika

Place potatoes in a large saucepan; add enough water to cover by one inch. Add one teaspoon salt to water. Bring to a boil over high heat; reduce heat to medium. Simmer for about 20 minutes, until fork-tender all the way through. Drain well; transfer potatoes to a large bowl. Run a knife through potatoes, cutting into bite-size pieces; set aside. In a small bowl, mix together mayonnaise, mustard, pickle juice, lemon juice and onion powder. Spoon over potatoes and mix in well. Add pickles, relish, celery, onion and eggs; mix well. Season with salt and pepper; sprinkle lightly with paprika. Cover with plastic wrap and refrigerate until serving time. Makes 8 servings.

A mini photo album is just right for keeping go-to recipes handy on the kitchen counter. Tuck in a few photos of happy family mealtimes too!

Favorite
Sides & Salads

Make & Take Mac Salad

Teresa Eller
Kansas City, KS

I made this macaroni salad for my mom because the storebought kind had way too much sodium. My niece came over for lunch and we had this salad with our ham sandwich. She said this was the best macaroni salad she had ever eaten in her entire life! I felt so honored and happy that my mom and niece loved my macaroni salad.

1 c. elbow macaroni, uncooked
4 eggs, hard-boiled, peeled
   and chopped
1 c. mayonnaise
3 green onions, chopped
2 T. mustard

1 T. celery salt
1 T. dried dill weed
1/4 c. celery, chopped
1/4 c. kosher baby dill
   pickles, chopped

Cook macaroni according to package directions; drain. Rinse with cold water; drain and transfer macaroni to a bowl with a tight-fitting lid. Add remaining ingredients; mix well. Cover and refrigerate until serving time. Makes 8 to 10 servings.

When fall days are too chilly to go outside, enjoy some family fun inside! Get out the crayons and coloring books, make your own paper dolls or have a picnic in front of the fireplace.

Harvest
for Sharing

Loretta's Yams

Norma Burton
Kuna, ID

My little sister has been making these yams for so many years. They're the dish we always count on for Thanksgiving and Christmas dinners.

2 lbs. yams or sweet potatoes,
    peeled and cut into chunks
2 eggs, beaten
3/4 c. sugar
1/2 c. plus 3 T. butter, softened
    and divided

1 t. vanilla extract
1/2 c. brown sugar, packed
1/4 c. all-purpose flour
1/2 c. chopped walnuts
    or pecans

In a large saucepan, cover yams or sweet potatoes with water. Cook over medium-high heat until fork-tender. Drain thoroughly; place in a large bowl. Add eggs, sugar, 1/2 cup butter and vanilla; beat with an electric mixer on medium speed until well blended. Spoon into a greased 1-1/2 quart casserole dish. For topping, mix together brown sugar, flour, nuts and remaining butter until crumbly. Sprinkle over yam mixture. Bake, uncovered, at 350 degrees for one hour, until bubbly and golden. Serves 6 to 8.

Host a family reunion this fall...the weather is almost always picture-perfect! When sending invitations, be sure to encourage everyone to bring photos, recipes, videos, scrapbooks and anything that inspires memories.

Warm &
Inviting
Soups

Harvest
for Sharing

Alphabet Soup

Kathy Grashoff
Fort Wayne, IN

Kids love this soup because it's yummy and fun. You'll love it because it's easy and packed with veggies!

1 T. butter
1 T. olive oil
1 c. baby carrots, sliced
1 c. onion, diced
1/2 c. celery, sliced
2 cloves garlic, minced
32-oz. container vegetable,
  chicken or beef broth
1 c. water

1/2 c. alphabet macaroni,
  uncooked
1 c. fresh spinach, torn
1 t. dried oregano or Italian
  seasoning
salt and pepper to taste
Optional: shredded Parmesan
  cheese

In a soup pot over medium heat, melt butter with olive oil. Add carrots, onion, celery and garlic; stir in broth and water. Bring to a simmer over medium heat; simmer for 10 minutes. Stir in macaroni and spinach; cook for 8 minutes, or until macaroni is tender and spinach is wilted. Stir in seasonings. Serve soup bowls topped with Parmesan cheese, if desired. Makes 4 servings.

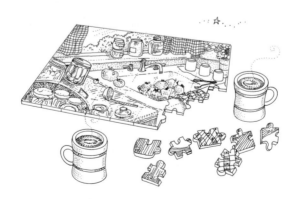

Family night! Serve a simple supper, then spend the evening assembling jigsaw puzzles or playing favorite board games together.

Warm & Inviting
Soups

Back-to-School Bread

Maegan Stauffer
Findlay, OH

Packed with pumpkin and spices, this bread just smells and tastes like fall! It was even a hit with my toddler, Carson. The recipe makes two loaves, so it's great for sharing.

3 c. all-purpose flour	1 t. salt
1/2 c. sugar	1 t. cinnamon
1 c. oil	1/2 t. ground ginger
3 eggs, beaten	1/4 t. ground cloves
1 t. baking powder	1 c. zucchini, shredded
1 t. baking soda	1/2 c. canned pumpkin

In a large bowl, mix all ingredients well. Divide batter between 2 greased 9"x5" loaf pans or 8"x8" baking pans. Bake at 350 degrees for 45 to 50 minutes. Allow to cool; turn out of pans and slice. Makes 2 loaves.

A wrapped loaf of homemade bread tied to a wooden cutting board makes a heartwarming gift.

Harvest
for Sharing

Jordan's Scarecrow Chili

Carolyn Deckard
Bedford, IN

Our family camps together for Halloween, and everyone is asked to bring a pitch-in dish that has a Halloween or pumpkin patch theme. The hungry bunch loves my granddaughter's thick chili. It has hearty flavor, but isn't too spicy.

1-1/2 lbs. ground beef
3/4 c. onion, chopped
2 stalks celery, chopped
46-oz. can tomato juice
28-oz. can diced tomatoes, drained
10-3/4 oz. can tomato soup
1/2 c. water

15-1/2 oz. can kidney beans, drained and rinsed
1 to 2 T. brown sugar, packed
2 T. chili powder
3 bay leaves
salt and pepper to taste
1 c. elbow macaroni, uncooked

In a Dutch oven over medium heat, cook beef with onion and celery until beef is no longer pink; drain. Stir in remaining ingredients except macaroni. Bring to a boil; reduce heat to medium-low. Cover and simmer for 30 minutes, stirring occasionally. Meanwhile, cook macaroni in a separate pan according to package directions; drain and stir into soup. Simmer for another 5 minutes, or until heated through. Discard bay leaves before serving. Makes 16 servings.

Quesadillas are quick and filling partners for a bowl of soup... a nice change from grilled cheese! Sprinkle a flour tortilla with shredded cheese, top with another tortilla and toast lightly in a skillet until the cheese melts. Cut into wedges and serve with salsa.

Warm & Inviting
Soups

Best Cheese Soup

Sandy Coffey
Cincinnati, OH

*Good on a crisp autumn day! Being a great-grandma now,
the kids say to me, "What's cooking, Gram the Great?" I sometimes
cook extra veggies ahead of time and add to the soup pot.*

1/2 c. butter
1/4 c. onion, minced
3/4 c. all-purpose flour
2 c. 2% milk

10-oz. pkg. frozen mixed
   vegetables, thawed
salt to taste
1 c. shredded Cheddar cheese

Melt butter in a saucepan over medium heat; add onion and sauté until tender. Remove from heat; sprinkle in flour. Gradually add milk, whisking constantly until smooth. Return to heat. Stir in vegetables; cook until soup is thickened. Season with salt; stir in cheese. Continue to cook until well blended. Serves 4 to 6.

Pantry Chili

Liz Waggoner
Pie Town, NM

I call this "Pantry Chili" because I usually have most of the ingredients on hand in my pantry. I developed this recipe for my husband, who isn't a big fan of spicy foods, but really enjoys this dish. The corn and olives take some of the bite out of the chiles and spices.

1 lb. ground beef
10-oz. can diced tomatoes with
   mild green chiles
15-oz. can ranch-style beans
15-oz. can tomato sauce
8-1/2 oz. can corn, drained

2-1/4 oz. can sliced black olives,
   drained
Optional: shredded cheese,
   chopped onions, crushed
   tortilla chips

Brown beef in a large stockpot over medium-high heat; drain. Add undrained tomatoes and beans, tomato sauce, corn and olives. Bring to a boil, stirring occasionally. Reduce heat to low. Cover and simmer for 30 minutes, stirring often. Garnish, if desired. Makes 4 to 6 servings.

Harvest
for Sharing

Courtney's Creamy Tomato Tortellini Soup

*Courtney Maisa
Emmett, ID*

Nothing says warm and cozy like a bowl of soup! As soon as fall hits, this is one of the house favorites. If you think you will have leftovers, I recommend cooking and storing the pasta separately from soup.

3/4 c. red onion, diced
4 cloves garlic, minced
1 sprig fresh rosemary
1 t. olive oil
4 c. chicken broth
2 14-1/2 oz. cans diced
    fire-roasted tomatoes
15-oz. can tomato sauce
1/2 c. whipping cream
1/4 t. salt

1/4 t. pepper
3 fresh basil leaves, sliced,
    or 1/2 t. dried basil
20-oz. pkg. 5-cheese tortellini,
    uncooked
1/2 c. shredded Parmesan cheese
Optional: additional shredded
    Parmesan cheese, ricotta
    cheese, fresh basil

In a large Dutch oven, combine onion, garlic, rosemary and olive oil. Sauté over medium heat for 6 to 8 minutes, until onion is translucent. Stir in chicken broth, tomatoes with juice, tomato sauce, cream, salt, pepper and basil. Bring to a boil; reduce heat to medium-low. Simmer for 20 minutes. Add tortellini; cook for 10 to 15 minutes, until tender and cooked through. Stir in Parmesan cheese; garnish as desired. Makes 8 servings.

Mmm...cheese! Golden cheese crisps are tasty with soups and salads. Spoon mounds of freshly shredded Parmesan cheese onto a parchment paper-lined baking sheet, 4 inches apart. Bake at 400 degrees for 5 to 7 minutes, until melted and golden. Cool and enjoy.

Bacon-Cheddar Bread

Joanne Novellino
Bayville, NJ

Pair this tasty bread with a bowl of hot soup or chili
for a wonderful cool-weather meal.

1-1/2 c. all-purpose flour
2 t. baking powder
1/2 t. kosher salt
1/2 t. pepper
2 eggs, beaten
1/2 c. buttermilk
1/2 c. butter, melted

1/3 c. grated Parmesan cheese
4 slices bacon, crisply cooked
　and crumbled
1/4 c. fresh chives or green
　onions, chopped
1-1/4 c. shredded sharp
　Cheddar cheese

In a large bowl, whisk together flour, baking powder, salt and pepper;
set aside. In another bowl, whisk together eggs, buttermilk and melted
butter; add to flour mixture and stir well. Fold in remaining ingredients.
Pour batter into an 8-1/2"x4-1/2" loaf pan sprayed with non-stick
spray. Bake at 350 degrees for about 45 minutes, until golden. Cool
loaf in pan; turn out of pan and slice. Makes one loaf.

The leaves fall, the wind blows,
and the farm country slowly changes from
the summer cottons into its winter wools.

–Henry Beston

Harvest
for Sharing

Unstuffed Cabbage Soup

*Sharon Jones
Fountain, FL*

This is the best healthy, delicious soup to have any night of the week, especially when it's cold outside. It can simmer for a few more minutes while you make grilled cheese sandwiches, if desired.

1 to 1-1/2 lbs. ground beef
2 14-1/2 oz. cans petite diced
   tomatoes
15-oz. can tomato sauce
1 head cabbage, chopped

3/4 c. onion, chopped
1 T. garlic, minced
1 T. Worcestershire sauce
salt and pepper to taste

Brown beef in a skillet over medium heat; drain. Meanwhile. combine remaining ingredients in a soup pot; bring to a boil. Add beef to boiling soup. Reduce heat to medium-low. Cover and simmer for 15 to 20 minutes, stirring often. Serves 6 to 8.

Crystal's Vegetarian Egg Drop Soup

*Tammy Pickering
Fairport, NY*

My daughter Crystal, being vegetarian, makes this soup to her liking. I love when she makes it for me when I visit her. It is so full of flavor... I have never tasted egg drop soup so delicious in any Asian restaurant.

6 c. plus 3 T. plus 2 t. water,
   divided
1 T. soy sauce
2 t. vegetable soup base

1 t. salt
1/2 t. sugar
1 T. cornstarch
6 to 8 eggs

In a large saucepan over medium heat, combine 6 cups water, soy sauce, soup base, salt and sugar; bring to a boil. Meanwhile, in a cup, mix cornstarch with 3 tablespoons water, making a paste. Add to hot broth in pan; mix well. In another bowl, beat eggs with remaining water. Add egg mixture to hot broth while stirring; cook and stir until eggs are set. Serves 5 to 6.

Warm & Inviting
Soups

Cheesy Chicken & Vegetable Soup
Sherry Page
Barberton, OH

This recipe is delicious and flexible...and it feeds a crowd! If you prefer, 6 to 8 chicken thighs may be used, or even a large can of chicken breast. Instead of noodles, 2 cups cooked rice may be added.

4 to 6 boneless, skinless
   chicken breasts
3 32-oz. containers
   chicken broth
15-1/4 oz. can corn
14-1/2 oz. can cut green beans

15-oz. can black beans, drained
1/2 t. cayenne pepper
salt and pepper to taste
2 c. thin egg noodles, uncooked
16-oz. pkg. pasteurized process
   cheese, cubed

In a large soup pot, cover chicken breasts with water. Simmer over medium heat until chicken is very tender; drain and set aside. In same soup pot, combine chicken broth, corn, all beans and seasonings; shred chicken and add to pot. Simmer over medium-low heat for 15 minutes, or until heated through. Stir in noodles; cook until tender. Fold in cheese cubes. Cook and stir until creamy and smooth. Makes 15 to 20 servings.

A friend who's under the weather will love it when you deliver a goodie basket to her door. Fill it with homemade soup and bread, a good book and a pair of fuzzy slippers. Just right for beating the fall sniffles!

Harvest
for Sharing

Harvest Black Bean &
Pumpkin Chili

Robbi Courtaway
Webster Groves, MO

*This chili tastes like autumn! It's surprisingly hearty for
a veggie chili, and is packed with good flavor.*

2 14-1/2 oz. cans petite
   diced tomatoes
2 15-1/2 oz. cans black beans,
   drained
1 c. canned pumpkin
3/4 c. onion, diced
1 T. chili powder

1 t. cinnamon
1 t. ground cumin
1/4 t. nutmeg
1/8 t. ground cloves
1/2 t. sea salt
1/2 t. coarse pepper

Add tomatoes with juice and remaining ingredients to a 4-quart slow
cooker; stir. Cover and cook on low setting for 8 to 10 hours. Stir again
before serving. Makes 8 servings.

When I was little, my family and I lived in Niagara Falls, New York.
We lived in an apartment complex made up of maybe 20 side-by-
side apartments. During the 60s and early 70s, Halloween was so
much fun and exciting. When we didn't have much money to buy
our costumes at the five & dime store, my dad would dress us up
in homemade costumes. On Halloween night, we would get tons of
candy, our pillow cases filled to the brim. I look back at those photos
of my brother and me and our friends, smiling about all the great
memories I have. I miss those days. Sometimes I wish I could go back
in time to relive them, so much excitement of how much "loot" we
would get, and who got the best chocolate bars and bubble gum.

–Sheila Galus, Mantua, OH

Corny Raisin Muffins

Sondra Keller
Naperville, IL

I've made this recipe for every Thanksgiving meal, forever...can't remember how many years! It travels well, and with only five ingredients, it's easy too. I usually double the recipe to avoid any possible bickering and minor squabbles over the last muffin.

1/2 c. raisins
1 c. boiling water
8-1/2 oz. pkg. corn muffin mix
1/4 c. butter, melted

8-3/4 oz. can cream-style corn
1/2 c. shredded sharp Cheddar
  cheese
Garnish: butter or honey butter

In a small bowl, combine raisins and boiling water; set aside until plump. Meanwhile, in a large bowl, prepare muffin mix according to package directions. Stir remaining ingredients except garnish into batter. Drain raisins well; pat dry and fold into batter. Scoop one inch of batter into each of 12 greased muffin cups. (Baked muffins will be muffin top size.) Bake at 400 degrees for 18 to 20 minutes. Allow to cool in pan. Transfer muffins to a serving plate and serve with butter or honey butter. Makes one dozen.

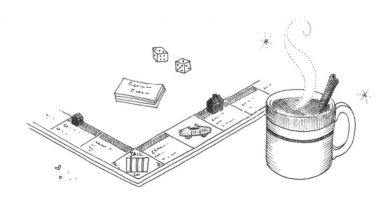

That first crackling fire and scent of wood smoke tell us it's fall! Gather lots of games and puzzles for cozy nights at home with family & friends.

Harvest
for Sharing

Mom's 7-Can Soup

Pat Addison
Cave Junction, OR

When the weather got chilly and Mom didn't have a whole lot of time to make soup, she made her "7-Can Soup" for us and we loved it. It tasted really good on cool fall days and warmed us up on fall weekends. I remember Dad just loved this soup too. Mom would double the recipe so Dad and his friends could enjoy hot soup, sandwiches and cold beer while watching football games. I still make this soup for my family every fall and winter.

15-1/2 oz. can fiesta corn and
    diced peppers
15-1/2 oz. can kidney beans
15-1/2 oz. can pinto beans
15-1/2 oz. can black beans
15-oz. can chili without beans

14-1/2 oz. can diced tomatoes
14-1/2 oz. can diced tomatoes
    with mild green chiles
salt and pepper to taste
8-oz. pkg. pasteurized process
    cheese, cubed

Combine all canned ingredients in a soup pot; do not drain. Bring to a boil over high heat; reduce heat to medium-low. Simmer for 10 to 15 minutes, stirring occasionally. Season with salt and pepper. Add cheese cubes; cook and stir until melted. Serves 6.

Instead of carving your pumpkin this year, why not paint it
in your favorite team's colors? You could even paint on
their logo or mascot. Spooky fun!

Warm & Inviting *Soups*

Hamburger Soup

Carla Tedford
Leavenworth, WA

Back in 1980, I tasted something similar to this soup while on a trip in Oregon, at a little back-road coffee shop. I came home and recreated the soup, and I have been making it regularly ever since. I like to serve it with cornmeal biscuits.

1 lb. ground beef
1 yellow onion, chopped
4 c. water
5 cubes beef bouillon
1 t. garlic powder

4 potatoes, peeled and cut into
   large cubes
1/2 head cabbage, shredded
16-oz. pkg. frozen corn, thawed

In a large soup pot over medium heat, brown beef with onion; drain. Add water, bouillon cubes and garlic powder; bring to a boil. Reduce heat to medium-low; cover and simmer for 30 minutes. Stir in potatoes and cabbage; continue simmering for 10 minutes. Add corn; cook until heated through and all vegetables are tender. Makes 8 to 10 servings.

When autumn weather is at its best, host a chili cook-off! Ask neighbors to bring a pot of their "secret recipe" chili to share, then have a friendly judging for the best. You can even hand out wooden spoons, oven mitts and aprons as prizes!

Colors of Fall Soup

Aqsa Masood
Ontario, Canada

I just love fall and all its colors, and I enjoy sharing this delicious warm soup with my family. We like to dip toasted, buttered bread in our soup...sometimes simple memories last forever! Top the soup with a sprinkle of diced hard-boiled eggs, if you like.

2 T. oil
1 c. frozen mixed vegetables
1-1/2 c. cooked chicken,
    shredded or diced
2 to 3 c. chicken broth
2 t. soy sauce

Optional: 1 t. sriracha sauce
1 t. salt, or to taste
1/2 t. pepper
2 T. cornstarch
3 to 4 T. cold water

Heat oil in a soup pot over medium heat. Add frozen vegetables and cook until partially tender. Add chicken; sauté until golden. Add chicken broth, sauces, salt and pepper; bring to a boil. Boil for 3 minutes. In a small bowl, stir together cornstarch and water. Stir into soup, a little at a time; cook to desired thickness. Makes 4 servings.

Tag sales and flea markets are the best places to find tea cups, mugs and even kid-size cups. Half the fun is mixing & matching colors and patterns for serving cider or cocoa... even cozy cups of hot soup!

Warm & Inviting
Soups

Vicky's Easy Homemade Bread

Vicky Tinnin
Peshtigo, WI

This is one of my family's favorite breads! You can do so much with this recipe. Add chopped herbs or sunflower seeds to the dough for different options...come up with your own ideas!

2 c. very warm water, about
   110 to 115 degrees
1/2 c. sugar
1-1/2 T. active dry yeast

1-1/2 t. salt
1/4 c. oil
6 c. all-purpose flour

Combine warm water and sugar in the bowl of an electric mixer. Stir until dissolved. Add yeast and let stand for several minutes, until foamy. Stir in salt and oil. With electric mixer on low to medium speed, mix in flour, one cup at a time. Knead dough with mixer's dough hook for about 7 minutes, allowing dough to pull from sides of bowl and form a ball. Spray another large bowl with non-stick vegetable spray; add dough and turn a few times to coat. Cover with plastic wrap and a clean tea towel; let rise until double. Push down dough and knead for about 5 minutes. Divide dough in half; shape into loaves and place in 2 greased 9"x5" loaf pans. Let rise for about 30 minutes, just until dough comes over the edge of pans. Bake at 350 degrees for 30 minutes. Makes 2 loaves.

Special Herb Butter

Sherry Page
Barberton, OH

Warm, home-baked breads call for scrumptious herb butter.

1 c. butter, softened
2 t. fresh flat-leaf parsley,
   chopped

2 t. fresh sage, chopped
2 t. fresh thyme, chopped

Stir together all ingredients in a small bowl until blended. Serve immediately, or cover and refrigerate up to 4 weeks. Makes about one cup.

Harvest
for Sharing

Zucchini & Italian Sausage Soup

Melanie Lowe
Dover, DE

A hearty, satisfying recipe that makes enough for a crowd!
Add some garlicky croutons or garlic toast.

19-1/2 oz. pkg. hot or sweet
    Italian pork sausage links,
    casings removed
3/4 c. onion, chopped
4 stalks celery, chopped
2 t. Italian seasoning
1 t. dried oregano
1/2 t. garlic powder
1/2 t. dried basil

1/2 t. salt
4 14-1/2 oz. cans no-salt-added
    whole tomatoes
14-1/2 oz. cans reduced-sodium
    chicken broth
2 to 3 zucchini, diced
2 green peppers, diced
1 t. sugar

In a large stockpot over medium heat, brown and crumble sausage,
about 5 to 7 minutes. Remove sausage to a bowl with a slotted spoon.
Add onion, celery and seasonings to drippings in same pot. Cook and
stir until onion is tender, about 4 to 6 minutes; drain. Stir in tomatoes
with juice and remaining ingredients; crush tomatoes with a spoon.
Return sausage to pot. Bring to a boil; reduce heat to medium-low.
Cover and simmer for about 30 minutes, stirring occasionally, until
vegetables are tender. Serves 10.

Decorate brown lunch bags with holes, using a paper punch.
Weight bags with a little sand and tuck in tea lights...
perfect for lighting the way to your next get-together!

Warm & Inviting
Soups

Creamy Italian Bean Soup

JoAnn
Gooseberry Patch

This soup will warm you through on a chilly day! Garnish with shredded Parmesan cheese and chunky crumbled bacon.

1 T. extra-virgin olive oil
1 onion, chopped
1 stalk celery, chopped
1 to 2 cloves garlic, minced
2 15-1/2 oz. cans cannellini
    beans, drained and rinsed

3 14-1/2 oz. cans chicken broth
1/4 t. dried marjoram
1/4 t. pepper
1 bunch fresh spinach, thinly
    sliced
1 T. lemon juice

Heat oil in a soup pot over medium heat. Add onion and celery; cook for 5 to 8 minutes, until tender. Add garlic; cook and stir for 30 seconds. Stir in beans, chicken broth and seasonings; bring to a boil. Reduce heat to medium-low and simmer for 15 to 20 minutes. Using a slotted spoon, set aside 2 cups beans from soup to a blender. Process on low speed until smooth; return to soup pot. Bring to a boil, stirring occasionally. Stir in spinach; cook and stir until spinach is wilted. Stir in lemon juice and serve. Makes 4 to 6 servings.

For a harvest centerpiece in a jiffy, tuck a bundle of dried wheat stalks from the craft store into a hollowed-out pumpkin.

Harvest
for Sharing

Roasted Garlic Soup

Monica Britt
Fairdale, WV

*This flavorful soup is one of the dishes I always serve on Halloween
at our family's "Vampire Dinner," after the kids finish
trick-or-treating. We love to sprinkle croutons on top.*

6 T. butter
1-1/2 c. onions, chopped
1 t. salt
1 t. pepper
2 T. fresh thyme, chopped

1/4 c. all-purpose flour
8 c. low-sodium chicken broth
1 c. whipping cream
salt and pepper to taste
2 T. fresh parsley, chopped

Prepare Roasted Garlic; set aside. Meanwhile, melt butter in a soup pot
over medium-high heat. Add onions, salt and pepper. Cook, stirring
often, for 4 minutes, or until softened. Stir in garlic pulp and thyme;
sprinkle with flour. Cook for about one minute, stirring to blend in flour.
Add chicken broth; increase heat to high and bring to a boil. Boil rapidly
for 10 minutes, stirring often, until slightly thickened. Working in
batches, transfer soup to a blender; process until puréed. Return soup
to pan; bring to a simmer over medium heat. Stir in cream; season with
additional salt and pepper. Garnish with parsley and serve. Serves 8.

Roasted Garlic:

4 whole heads garlic   3 T. olive oil

Cut 1/4-inch off the top of each garlic head. Place garlic cut-side up
on an aluminum foil-lined baking sheet; drizzle with olive oil. Bake at
375 degrees for 45 minutes, or until softened. Cool enough to handle;
squeeze soft cooked pulp from each clove into a small bowl. Makes
about 1/2 cup pulp.

Warm & Inviting
Soups

Dilly Bread

Becky Myers
Ashland, OH

This bread is an old favorite that goes well with any kind of soup or stew...you can't eat just one slice. Pass the butter, please!

1/4 c. water
1 c. small-curd cottage cheese, warmed
1 egg, beaten
1/4 t. baking soda
1 t. salt
2 T. sugar
1 T. butter, melted
2 t. dried dill weed
1 T. dried, minced onions
2-1/2 c. all-purpose flour
2-1/2 t. active dry yeast

Add all ingredients to a bread machine in the order given in manufacturer's directions. Process as directed. (May also combine ingredients in a large bowl; beat with an electric mixer, using a dough hook.) Turn out dough; knead several times and place in a separate greased bowl. Cover with a clean tea towel; let rise until double. Transfer dough to a greased 8"x4-1/2" loaf pan; let rise again until double. Bake at 350 degrees about 40 minutes, or until a cooking thermometer inserted in the center reads 195 degrees. Makes one loaf.

When you start getting older, you tend to reflect on your childhood memories more often. I was raised on a farm in a holler and it was the best times of my life. I grew up with four cousins and we had a ball doing all kinds of things. Life was hard...we were not rich by any means. We made molasses, baled hay, cared for our horses, cows and chickens, raised tobacco and corn. We had taffy pulls, waded in the creek and played in the spring house. We ran all over the farm until it got dark and we knew it was time to get back to the house. Boy, did we have it made! I look at kids nowadays. They hold a phone in one hand and another gadget in the other. We never had all that technology and I can say that we all were better off without it! Those days will never be here again. Oh, how I miss those days.

–Tina Goodpasture, Meadowview, VA

Harvest
for Sharing

Smashed Potato Soup

Shannon Reents
Lexington, OH

A real comfort food...perfect for a simple autumn meal,
and ready to serve in a jiffy!

20-oz. pkg. refrigerated
   mashed potatoes
14-1/2 oz. can chicken broth
1/2 c. baby carrots, diced
1/2 c. celery, diced
1 clove garlic, minced
1/4 t. salt

1/8 t. pepper
1/2 c. sour cream
1/2 c. milk
2 T. fresh parsley, snipped
Garnish: shredded Cheddar
   cheese, crumbled bacon,
   snipped fresh chives

Spoon mashed potatoes into a large saucepan over medium heat. Gradually whisk in chicken broth until mixture is smooth. Stir in carrots, celery, garlic, salt and pepper; bring to a boil. Reduce heat to medium-low; simmer for 10 minutes. Remove from heat; stir in sour cream, milk and parsley. Ladle soup into bowls; garnish as desired. Makes 4 servings.

Ladle individual portions of leftover soup into small freezer bags... seal, label and freeze. Then, when you need a quick-fix lunch or dinner, simply transfer soup to a microwave-safe bowl and reheat.

Warm & Inviting
Soups

Oats & Cereal Flatbread

Peter Stadelman
Williamsville, NY

Cold and rainy day out? Bake up this delicious flatbread while your favorite soup is simmering.

2 c. whole-grain rice flake cereal,
    finely crushed
2 c. quick-cooking oats,
    uncooked
2 c. all-purpose flour

1/2 to 1 c. sugar
1 c. butter
3/4 c. warm water
1 t. baking soda

In a bowl, mix together cereal, oats, flour and sugar; cut in butter as for pie crust. Set aside. Combine warm water and baking soda in a cup; stir well and add to flour mixture. Mix well. Cover and refrigerate for several hours to overnight. Before baking, let dough stand at room temperature for about one hour. Roll out thinly on a floured surface; cut with with a round cookie cutter. If dough begins to get dry or crumbly, mix in a few drops of water. Arrange on lightly greased baking sheets. Bake at 350 degrees for 5 to 7 minutes. Makes about one dozen.

Fill mini jelly jars with candy corn and set a tealight inside each one. Their sweet glow will make the prettiest place settings!

Fiesta Chicken Soup

Vickie
Gooseberry Patch

*This soup is hearty, flavorful and easy...you'll be ladling it up
in no time at all! I like to garnish it with sliced avocado.*

10-3/4 oz. can fiesta nacho
  cheese soup
10-3/4 oz. can cream of
  chicken soup
2-2/3 c. milk
12-1/2 oz. can shredded white
  chicken, drained

10-oz. can enchilada sauce
15-1/2 oz. can black beans,
  drained and rinsed
4-oz. can diced green chiles
1 c. frozen corn
Garnish: sour cream, snipped
  fresh cilantro, tortilla chips

In a large saucepan, whisk together soups and milk. Add remaining
ingredients except garnish; stir well. Simmer over medium heat for
10 to 15 minutes until heated through, stirring often. Garnish as
desired. Makes 4 to 6 servings.

Crunchy tortilla strips are a tasty addition to southwestern-style
soups. Cut corn tortillas into thin strips, then deep-fry quickly.
Drain on paper towels before sprinkling over bowls of soup.
Try red or blue tortillas too!

Warm & Inviting
Soups

Southern Buttermilk Cornbread
Vivian Marshall
Columbus, OH

This Deep South-style cornbread is great, served with a hot bowl of bean soup. This was my grandmother's recipe and it's just absolutely the best! My part-Cherokee grandmother lived with my grandfather and their eleven youngin's in Hayesville, North Carolina, in a small log cabin that Grandfather had built. He farmed the land, and she and the children did the chores.

1/2 c. butter	1/2 t. baking soda
2/3 c. sugar	1 c. yellow cornmeal
2 eggs, beaten	1 c. all-purpose flour
1 c. buttermilk	1 t. salt
4 t. mayonnaise	

Melt butter in a cast-iron skillet over medium heat. Remove from heat; stir in sugar. Quickly add eggs and beat until well blended; set aside. Combine buttermilk, mayonnaise and baking soda in a bowl; mix well and stir into mixture in skillet. Stir in cornmeal, flour and salt until well-blended and just a few lumps remain. If skillet isn't oven-proof, pour batter into a greased 8" round baking pan. Bake at 375 degrees for 30 to 40 minutes, until a toothpick inserted in the center comes out clean. Immediately slice and serve warm. Makes 6 to 8 servings.

Grandma's old cast-iron skillet is perfect for baking crisp, delicious cornbread. Before you mix up the batter, add a tablespoon of bacon drippings or oil to the skillet and place it in the oven to preheat. When the batter is ready, the skillet will be too.

Harvest
for Sharing

Tasty Beef & Vegetable Soup

*Laura Flood
Markleville, IN*

Good old-fashioned vegetable soup! I think cooking the roast ahead of time makes this soup taste even better. It's delicious and makes plenty for sharing with family & friends.

3 to 4-lb. beef chuck roast
1/2 c. butter
2 to 3 T. ranch seasoning mix
4 c. water, divided
3 potatoes, peeled and diced
3 carrots, peeled and diced
2 c. canned crushed tomatoes
32-oz. bottle tomato juice

2 14-1/2 oz. cans cut green
   beans, drained
1/2 of a 10-oz. pkg. frozen peas
   & carrots
2 T. dried, minced onions
2 cubes beef bouillon
salt and pepper to taste

The evening before, place roast in a 6-quart slow cooker; add butter, seasoning mix and 2 cups water. Cover and cook on low setting for 8 hours or overnight, until roast is very tender. Remove roast to a bowl, reserving broth in slow cooker. (If preferred, cook roast the day before; refrigerate roast and broth separately.) Shred roast; add to reserved broth along with remaining water and other ingredients. Stir well. Cover and cook on low setting for 7 to 8 hours. Makes 8 to 10 servings.

A soup supper in front of a crackling fire...how cozy! Invite friends to bring their favorite veggies and cook up a big pot of hearty soup together. While the soup simmers, you can catch up on conversation.

Warm & Inviting
Soups

Quick White Chicken Chili

Constance Lewis
Florence, AL

*This is our go-to meal whenever we're watching football
on television...just add some tortilla chips!*

48-oz. jar Great Northern beans,
  drained and rinsed
12-1/2 oz. can shredded white
  chicken, drained
1-1/4 to 2 c. chicken broth
4-oz. can chopped green chiles
1 T. dried, chopped onions

1 c. sour cream
1 c. shredded Monterey
  Jack cheese
2 T. fresh cilantro or parsley,
  minced
Optional: additional sour cream

In a large saucepan, combine beans, chicken, chicken broth, chiles and
onions; stir well. Bring to a boil over medium-high heat; reduce heat to
low. Add sour cream, shredded cheese and cilantro; cook and stir until
cheese is melted. If desired, serve topped with additional sour cream.
Makes 6 to 8 servings.

Herb Biscuit Knots

Edward Kielar
Whitehouse, OH

Tasty and oh-so easy to make.

12-oz. tube refrigerated
  buttermilk biscuits,
  cut in half
1/2 c. canola oil

1/2 t. Italian seasoning
1/2 t. garlic powder
1/8 t. salt

Roll each biscuit piece into a 6-inch rope and tie into a loose knot.
Arrange biscuits on a greased baking sheet. Bake at 400 degrees for
9 to 11 minutes, until golden. Combine oil and seasonings in a small
bowl; brush over warm biscuits and serve. Makes 10 biscuits.

All seasons sweet, but autumn best of all.
–Elinor Wylie

Harvest
for Sharing

Lori's Fall Chowder

Lori Rosenberg
Cleveland, OH

After we have been out raking leaves, on a fall hike or other outdoor activity, this chowder is the perfect end to a great fall day. Served with a hearty bread, it is a meal that will carry you over to dinner.

1/2 lb. sliced bacon, sliced
   1/2-inch thick
1 T. butter
1 c. sweet onion, chopped
3 to 4 carrots, peeled and
   chopped
3 stalks celery, chopped
6 potatoes, peeled and diced
10-oz. pkg. frozen chopped
   broccoli, thawed

2 cloves garlic, finely chopped
1 t. paprika
1/4 t. red pepper flakes
salt and pepper to taste
3 c. chicken broth
1 c. half-and-half
Garnish: sliced green onions,
   garlic & cheese flavored
   croutons

In a Dutch oven or large saucepan, cook bacon over medium heat until crisp, 5 to 6 minutes. Transfer bacon to a paper towel-lined plate. Add butter to drippings in pan; add onion, carrots and celery. Cook until soft, stirring occasionally, about 5 to 7 minutes. Add potatoes, broccoli, garlic, paprika and pepper flakes; season with salt and pepper. Cook another 5 minutes. Stir in chicken broth and half-and-half; bring to a boil. Stir in bacon, or reserve for topping soup. Reduce heat to medium-low; simmer for 20 to 30 minutes. Ladle chowder into bowls; add desired toppings and serve. Makes 4 servings.

I am grateful for what I am and have.
My thanksgiving is perpetual.
   –Henry David Thoreau

Warm & Inviting
Soups

Pumpkin Patch Biscuits

Donna Wilson
Maryville, TN

These biscuits are wonderful and smell so good while baking. They go well with all kinds of soup and chili. My family loves them!

2 c. all-purpose flour
1/2 c. brown sugar, packed
2-1/2 t. baking powder
1/2 t. baking soda
1/2 t. salt

1/2 c. butter, chilled
3/4 c. canned pumpkin
1/2 c. buttermilk
1 t. butter, melted

In a large bowl, combine flour, brown sugar, baking powder, baking soda and salt; mix well. Cut in butter with a fork until mixture resembles crumbs. Combine pumpkin and buttermilk in a separate bowl; stir into flour mixture until dough forms. Turn out dough onto a lightly floured surface; roll into one-inch thickness. Cut with a floured biscuit cutter and place on a greased baking sheet. Bake at 425 degrees for 18 to 20 minutes. Remove from oven; brush with melted butter and serve warm. Makes one dozen.

Here in Florida, fall doesn't always come around on schedule! So, once the air is a little less humid and there's a hint of a chill, my family loves to go to a local family-run, faith-based pumpkin patch. They charge a small fee to help offset the cost of offering a huge, absolutely beautiful pumpkin patch with an assortment of varieties to choose from. They also have a hayride, a corn maze, a sunflower patch and plenty of areas created for family pictures. It is one of my favorite places to use as a backdrop for fall photos and a day out with my husband and kids. At the end of the season, the farm donates pumpkins to a local food pantry in town. We like to get back to the basics, with a big ol' pot of chili or stew and a backyard bonfire, toasting marshmallows and making s'mores together.

–Kristy Wells, Ocala, FL

Harvest
for Sharing

Turkey, Dressing & Dumpling Soup

Janis Parr
Ontario, Canada

This soup is hearty and delicious, like Thanksgiving dinner in a bowl...comfort food at its best.

2-lb. bone-in turkey breast,
    thawed if frozen
10 c. water
3 carrots, peeled and chopped
1 c. celery, chopped
1/2 c. onion, chopped

2 t. seasoned salt
1 t. salt
1/4 t. pepper
1-1/2 t. dried sage
1-1/4 t. poultry seasoning

Place turkey breast in a large soup pot. Add water, vegetables, salts and pepper; stir gently. Bring to a boil over medium-high heat. Reduce heat to medium-low; cover and simmer for 1-1/2 hours. Remove turkey to a bowl and let cool; cut into cubes, discarding skin and bones. Return turkey to soup. Stir in sage and poultry seasoning; bring to a boil for 10 minutes. Reduce heat. Drop Dumplings by large spoonfuls into hot soup. Simmer for 10 minutes. Cover and continue cooking until dumplings test done with a toothpick. Makes 8 to 10 servings.

Dumplings:

2 c. all-purpose flour
4 t. baking powder

1 t. salt
1 c. milk

Whisk together flour, baking powder and salt; stir in milk until combined. Mixture will be thick.

Save time when baking! Tuck a measuring cup into your countertop canisters...ready to scoop out flour and sugar in a jiffy.

Warm & Inviting
Soups

Creamy Corn Chowder

Kathy Grashoff
Fort Wayne, IN

A perfect way to enjoy the last of the summer sweet corn. Sometimes I'll choose Yukon Gold potatoes for their buttery color.

2 slices bacon, diced
4 ears sweet corn, kernels cut
    off, or 10-oz. pkg. frozen
    corn, thawed
5 new potatoes, peeled and diced
2 stalks celery, diced

1 carrot, peeled and diced
1/2 yellow onion, diced
4 c. chicken broth
1 c. whipping cream
salt and pepper to taste

Cook bacon in a stockpot over medium heat for about 8 minutes, until crisp. Add all vegetables and chicken broth; stir well. Increase heat to high; bring to a boil. Reduce heat to medium-low. Simmer for about 20 minutes, until vegetables are tender, stirring in cream when vegetables are nearly done. Season with salt and pepper. Ladle into soup mugs and serve. Makes 6 to 8 servings.

David's Taco Soup

David Kerr
Davison, MI

This recipe is so handy for an easy family dinner. I've brought it to potlucks at work as well...it was a huge hit! Leftovers can easily be reheated for a quick lunch.

1 lb. ground beef
1 onion, diced
1-1/4 oz. pkg. taco
    seasoning mix
14-1/2 oz. can diced tomatoes

15-1/4 oz. can corn
2 15-1/2 oz. cans kidney beans
1 c. water
Garnish: sour cream, shredded
    Cheddar cheese, tortilla chips

Brown beef with onion in a skillet over medium heat; drain. Stir in taco seasoning; transfer to a 4-quart slow cooker. Add undrained vegetables, beans and water; mix well. Cover and cook on low setting for 6 to 8 hours. Serve with sour cream, cheese and tortilla chips. Serves 5.

Quick Chicken Posole

Mary Garcia
Phoenix, AZ

My husband loves to put this together for football Saturdays, when his friends come over. It's hearty and filling. He sets out lots of toppings like sour cream, lime wedges, avocado slices and a big basket of tortilla chips.

2 lbs. boneless, skinless
    chicken thighs
1 t. ground cumin
1 t. chili powder
1 t. salt
1 t. pepper
2 T. olive oil
1 onion, diced
2 carrots, peeled and diced
2 stalks celery, diced

4 cloves garlic, minced
8 c. chicken broth
2 15-1/2 oz. cans hominy,
    drained and rinsed
14-1/2 oz. can diced tomatoes
    with green chiles
1 canned chipotle in adobo
    sauce, finely chopped
2 T. adobo sauce

Sprinkle both sides of chicken thighs with seasonings; set aside. Heat oil in a large soup pot over medium heat. Add chicken and brown on both sides. Remove chicken to a plate; reserve drippings in pan. Add onion, carrots, celery and garlic to pan; sauté for about 10 minutes, until softened. Add remaining ingredients; bring to a boil. Shred chicken and return to pan. Reduce heat to medium-low; simmer for 30 minutes. Serves 6 to 8.

Dress up south-of-the-border soups and dishes with a dollop of tangy Mexican crema. Look for it in the refrigerated section of the grocery. Your taste buds will say olé!

Warm & Inviting
Soups

Cheesy Potato Soup

Carole Schievelbein
Seguin, TX

I always make a big pot of this soup, because I like to give it as a gift. However, it would be easy to halve the recipe. It freezes well. I always use canned potato soup in this, rather than fresh potatoes...otherwise, it just doesn't taste as good!

1/2 c. butter
5 stalks celery, finely chopped
6 carrots, peeled and finely
   grated
1 c. onion, finely chopped
5 10-1/2 oz. cans chicken broth

5 10-3/4 oz. cans cream of
   potato soup
32-oz. pkg. pasteurized process
   cheese, cubed
16-oz. container sour cream
salt and pepper to taste

Melt butter in a large soup pot over medium heat. Sauté celery, carrots and onion for 5 to 6 minutes. Add chicken broth; simmer over medium-high heat for about 30 minutes. Fold in potato soup; do not stir, to avoid breaking up potatoes in soup. Simmer for 5 minutes. Turn off heat; fold in cheese until melted. Remove from heat; let cool slightly. Fold in sour cream; season with salt and pepper. Makes 12 servings.

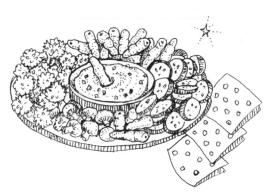

Whip up this super-simple veggie dip! Blend one cup cottage cheese, 1/4 cup plain Greek yogurt, one tablespoon minced onion, one teaspoon dried parsley and 1/4 teaspoon dill weed. Serve with bite-size fresh vegetables...a great go-with for soup & sandwich suppers.

Harvest
for Sharing

Broccoli-Cheddar Potato Soup

*Charlotte Smith
Huntingdon, PA*

*This is a great recipe for a chilly day...someone is
always coming back for seconds!*

1 T. butter
3/4 c. onion, chopped
1/2 c. carrot, peeled and chopped
2 stalks celery, chopped
2 cloves garlic, minced
2 T. all-purpose flour
salt and pepper to taste

2-1/2 c. chicken broth
1 c. milk
2 russet potatoes, peeled and
    cubed
4 c. broccoli flowerets
1 T. grated Parmesan cheese
1 c. shredded Cheddar cheese

Melt butter in a large saucepan over medium heat. Add onion, carrot,
celery and garlic; cook and stir for 5 minutes. Add flour, salt and pepper;
stir well. Add chicken broth, milk and potatoes; bring to a boil. Simmer
over low heat for 15 minutes, Add broccoli and Parmesan cheese; cook
and stir for 5 minutes. Add Cheddar cheese; stir well and remove from
heat. Remove 2 cups of soup mixture to a blender; process until smooth.
Return to saucepan. Stir well. Simmer for 30 to 45 minutes, until
vegetables are tender. Serves 8.

Crunchy toppings can really add fun and flavor to bowls of soup.
Some good choices are cheesy fish crackers, French fried onions,
bacon bits, sunflower seeds and toasted nuts. Check the pantry...
you're sure to find a few!

Homestead Oatmeal Bread

Janis Parr
Ontario, Canada

This is a dense, hearty and delicious loaf, perfect to serve with a steaming hot bowl of soup or stew. I've been known to make a meal out of this bread alone! It makes great toast and freezes well too.

3-3/4 c. all-purpose flour
1 c. plus 1 t. quick-cooking oats, uncooked and divided
1-1/4 t. granular active dry yeast
1 t. salt
2 T. honey
2 c. plus 3 T. very warm water, about 110 to 115 degrees
1 t. vanilla extract

In a large bowl, combine flour, one cup oats, yeast and salt; stir well and set aside. In a small bowl, dissolve honey in hot water; stir in vanilla. Let cool slightly; add to flour mixture. Stir until all flour is mixed into the dough. Cover bowl with plastic wrap; let stand at room temperature for 12 to 24 hours. When ready to bake, line a Dutch oven with parchment paper, cutting paper large enough to fit into the bottom of pan and up the sides. Add lid; preheat in oven at 450 degrees. Meanwhile, shape dough into a round on a floured surface. Make a few slashes across the top with a sharp knife; sprinkle with remaining oats. Carefully remove hot Dutch oven from oven; place dough onto parchment paper in pan. Add lid and bake at 450 degrees for 30 minutes. Uncover; return to oven for 20 minutes, or until lightly golden. Remove from oven. Allow to cool before slicing. Store bread in a plastic zipping bag or covered container. Makes one loaf.

Keep a warm quilt or blanket-stitched throw in the car for autumn picnics and football games...perfect for keeping warm and cozy.

Harvest
for Sharing

Pumpkin Spice Bisque

*Mary Jefferson Rabon
Mobile, AL*

*This is amazing if you love pumpkin and spice! A soup with
a sweet taste, and just so comforting for fall cool nights.*

2 15-oz. cans pumpkin
1/4 to 1/2 c. sugar, to taste
2 t. cinnamon
1 t. ground ginger
1/2 t. ground cloves

1 t. nutmeg
3 12-oz. cans evaporated milk
3 eggs, beaten
Garnish: whipped cream, nutmeg

Combine pumpkin, sugar and spices in a large saucepan; stir in
evaporated milk. Heat through over medium-low heat, stirring
constantly. Gradually stir in beaten eggs until well mixed and set.
Garnish bowls of soup with a dollop of whipped cream and a sprinkle
of nutmeg. Makes 10 to 12 servings.

Pineapple Cornmeal Muffins

*Joyce Roebuck
Jacksonville, TX*

Yummy with soups, or for breakfast.

3/4 c. yellow cornmeal
1 c. all-purpose flour
1 T. baking powder
2-1/2 T. sugar
1/4 t. salt

1 egg, beaten
2/3 c. pineapple juice
3 T. shortening, melted
1/2 c. crushed pineapple, drained

In a bowl, mix together cornmeal, flour, baking powder, sugar and salt;
set aside. In another bowl, beat together egg and pineapple juice; stir
in flour mixture. Stir in shortening and pineapple; mix well but do not
overbeat. Spoon batter into greased muffin cups, filling 2/3 full. Bake
at 400 degrees for 20 to 25 minutes, until lightly golden. Makes 8 to
10 muffins.

Feasts for
Family &
Friends

Harvest
for Sharing

Autumn Fiesta Chicken Casserole

Janet Teas
Zanesville, OH

This is a good, warming casserole for a chilly autumn evening.

2 c. wide egg noodles, uncooked
1/2 c. onion, chopped
1/2 c. green pepper, chopped
1 T. canola oil
10-3/4 oz. can fiesta nacho
   cheese soup

1/2 c. whole milk
1 t. salt
1/8 t. pepper
6-oz. pkg. shredded cooked
   chicken
1/2 c. tortilla chips, crushed

Cook noodles according to package directions; drain. Meanwhile, in a large skillet over medium heat, sauté onion and green pepper in canola oil until tender. Stir in cheese soup, milk, salt and pepper; bring to a boil. Fold in cooked noodles and shredded chicken. Transfer mixture to a lightly greased 2-quart casserole dish; sprinkle with crushed tortilla chips. Bake, uncovered, at 350 degrees for 25 to 30 minutes, until hot and bubbly. Serves 4.

Feeding a crowd? Serve festive Mexican or Italian-style dishes that everybody loves. They're often served with rice or pasta, so they're filling yet budget-friendly. The theme makes it a snap to put together the menu and table decorations too.

Feasts for
Family & Friends

Kielbasa & Cabbage

Joan Thamsen
Conway, SC

This is a great dish that can be served as a main, brunch or appetizer. Perfect on any buffet table...a great addition to an autumn football party. This recipe can be doubled or tripled if you want to...can be frozen and reheated, too.

1/4 c. butter
3/4 c. onion, chopped
2 McIntosh apples, cored
    and cubed
1 head cabbage, cut into
    1-inch pieces

1 lb. Kielbasa sausage, cut into
    1-inch chunks
Optional: 12-oz. pkg. mini
    Cheddar pierogies, uncooked
Optional: additional butter

Melt butter in a large skillet over medium heat. Add onion and apples; sauté until soft. Add cabbage; continue cooking until softened and cooked down. Meanwhile, place sausage in an ungreased shallow baking pan. Bake, uncovered, at 350 degrees for 25 minutes, or until browned. Add sausage to cabbage mixture in skillet. If desired, cook pierogies according to package directions, just until tender; drain and fold into cabbage mixture. Simmer over low heat for 30 to 40 minutes, until flavors are blended, adding more butter if desired. Makes 4 to 6 servings.

Create a warm glow using box graters picked up at flea markets. The more character, the better, so look for ones that have darkened with age and are even a bit worn. Pick up a variety of sizes and tuck tea lights inside. So simple!

Harvest
for Sharing

Mom's Classic Meatloaf

Jane Ivey
Winterville, GA

My mother has always made this meatloaf in the fall, when it begins to get cold outside. It's delicious with steamed rice or mashed potatoes and green beans. Instead of the bread, 1/2 cup cracker crumbs or dry bread crumbs may be used.

2 slices white bread, torn
2 lbs. ground beef
2 eggs, beaten
1/3 c. rolled oats, uncooked
1/3 c. catsup
2 T. Worcestershire sauce
1/2 c. onion, finely chopped

Optional: 1 green pepper,
  finely chopped
3/4 c. shredded Mexican-blend
  cheese
garlic salt, salt and pepper
  to taste

Place bread in a large bowl; add enough water to moisten bread and squeeze out. Add remaining ingredients; mix well and shape into a loaf. Place in an aluminum foil-lined 13"x9" deep baking pan coated with non-stick vegetable spray. Bake, uncovered, at 375 degrees for about 45 minutes; check for doneness. Slice and serve. Makes 8 to 10 servings.

I was born and raised in Florida so, as a child, autumn was only something I would see in pictures. Leaves changing colors, full moons and kids jumping in piles of leaves were always just a dream. Though there were some exciting signs of fall, like seeing hundreds of birds flying in the sky making their way to warmth, I longed to know what it was really like. When I was 30 we moved to northeast Ohio and have lived here now for nearly 30 years. Fall is my favorite time. We have bonfires, roast marshmallows, pick pumpkins from the patch, go on hikes in the woods, bake and eat lots of fall favorites! Now if I could just have the beach nearby, all would be perfect!

–Suzette Rummell, Cuyahoga Falls, OH

Feasts for
Family & Friends

Easy Chili Con Carne

Shirley Howie
Foxboro, MA

I have been using this recipe for years now. It's easy to put together, and there's enough left over for my hubby and me to have another bowl the next day! I like to serve it with warm cornbread.

2 T. butter
1 onion, chopped
1 lb. lean ground beef
1 clove garlic, minced
2 10-oz. cans diced tomatoes
    with green chiles

15-1/2 oz. can kidney beans,
    drained and rinsed
1 T. chili powder
1 t. salt
1/2 t. pepper

Melt butter in a large saucepan over medium heat; add onion and sauté until soft. Add beef and cook until browned; drain. Add garlic and cook for one minute longer. Add tomatoes with juice, beans and seasonings; stir well. Cover and simmer over medium-low heat for one hour, stirring occasionally. Serves 4.

Baja-Style Chicken Bowls

Annette Ingram
Grand Rapids, MI

My kids love this easy dish for busy-day suppers! Leftover roast turkey can be used instead of chicken. Black beans are good too.

4 t. olive oil
1-1/4 c. cooked chicken, cubed
1 c. frozen corn, thawed
1 to 2 red peppers, sliced
1 c. favorite chunky salsa

salt and pepper to taste
2 c. cooked brown rice, warmed
3/4 c. shredded Monterey
    Jack cheese

Heat oil in a skillet over medium heat. Add chicken, corn and red pepper; cook and stir until heated through and red pepper is crisp-tender, about 5 minutes. Stir in salsa; season with salt and pepper. Divide cooked rice among 3 to 4 shallow soup bowls; top with chicken mixture. Top with cheese and serve. Makes 3 to 4 servings.

Artichoke Spaghetti

Anna Frioli
Belleair Beach, FL

Growing up in an Italian family, we always ate a lot of pasta. But one day, I was craving something other than the usual red sauce over spaghetti. This meatless pasta dish combines simple ingredients to make a creamy sauce that goes perfectly with artichokes and olives. Buon appetito!

16-oz. pkg. spaghetti, uncooked
1/4 c. butter
7 T. olive oil, divided
2 T. all-purpose flour
1 c. vegetable broth

1 T. dried parsley
14-oz. can artichoke hearts,
   drained and cut in half
2/3 c. sliced black olives, drained
1/4 c. grated Parmesan cheese

Cook spaghetti according to package directions; drain. Meanwhile, melt butter in a saucepan; blend in 1/4 cup olive oil. Add flour; cook and stir until smooth. Gradually stir in vegetable broth; cook for one minute, or until thickened. Add parsley. Cook for 5 minutes, stirring constantly. Add artichokes, olives and cheese to sauce. Cover and simmer for 5 minutes. To serve, toss cooked spaghetti with remaining olive oil. Transfer spaghetti to a serving bowl and spoon sauce over spaghetti. Makes 4 to 6 servings.

Set a regular dinner theme for each night of the week...
Spaghetti Night, Taco Night or Soup & Salad Night,
based on your family's favorites. You'll be creating
memories together, and meal planning is a snap!

Feasts for
Family & Friends

Baked Cavatini

Kathy Grashoff
Fort Wayne, IN

With three kinds of pasta, this dish is just like the baked pasta we all remember from a favorite pizza chain's menu. It makes a delicious dinner and is a great way to use up odds & ends of pasta in the cupboard. Just add a tossed salad and dinner is ready.

1-1/2 c. spiral pasta, uncooked
1-1/2 c. macaroni shells,
   uncooked
1-1/2 c. elbow macaroni,
   uncooked
1/2 lb. mild Italian ground
   pork sausage
1/2 lb. ground beef

3/4 c. onion, diced
1 green pepper, diced
4-oz. can sliced mushrooms,
   drained
40-oz. jar spaghetti sauce
3 c. shredded Italian-blend or
   mozzarella cheese, divided

Cook pastas together according to package directions, just until tender; drain. Meanwhile, in a large skillet over medium heat, brown sausage and beef with onion and green pepper; drain well. Stir in mushrooms, sauce and 2 cups cheese; fold in cooked pasta. Transfer to a greased 13"x9" baking pan; sprinkle with remaining cheese. Cover and bake at 350 degrees for 30 to 40 minutes, until hot and bubbly. Makes 4 to 6 servings.

Host a recipe swap! Invite friends to bring a favorite casserole
along with enough recipe cards for each guest. While everyone
enjoys a delicious potluck, collect the recipe cards, staple
together and hand out when it's time to depart.

Harvest
for Sharing

Super-Easy Chicken Cacciatore *Denise Underwood*
Cincinnati, OH

The grocers had a huge sale on chicken thighs and because I share the kitchen with my grandmother, freezing space is limited. So while I was at the store, I decided I would cook them all at once and make Chicken Cacciatore. This is what I came up with...it was delicious! Serve over cooked thin spaghetti or rice, with hot garlic bread.

2 T. oil
8 chicken thighs
salt and pepper to taste
24-oz. jar favorite pasta sauce
12-oz. pkg. frozen 3-pepper & onion blend, thawed
0.7-oz. pkg. Italian salad dressing mix

1 c. red wine or chicken broth
6-oz. jar sliced mushrooms, drained
6-oz. can whole black olives, drained and halved

Heat oil in a large skillet over medium high. Season chicken thighs on both sides with salt and pepper; add to skillet. Cook chicken for 8 minutes on each side, until golden. Remove chicken to a bowl; set aside to cool. Combine remaining ingredients in a stockpot; stir well and bring to a low boil over medium heat. Cut chicken into cubes and add to pan. Reduce heat to medium-low and simmer for one hour, stirring occasionally. Serves 4 to 6.

Boneless chicken breasts and thighs cook up faster if pounded thin with a meat mallet or even a small heavy skillet. Place meat in a large plastic zipping bag first for no-mess convenience.

Feasts for Family & Friends

Dutch Oven Parmesan Chicken

Marian Forck
Chamois, MO

We love making this in the Dutch oven! Sometimes we add potatoes and they will bake while the chicken is cooking. We used to make it when we went camping, but those days are gone. Now we make it at home on a Saturday night and it's still tasty.

1 T. olive oil
1/3 c. butter, melted
1-1/2 c. grated Parmesan cheese
1/4 t. pepper

garlic powder to taste
3 lbs. boneless, skinless
    chicken tenders

Prepare a campfire with plenty of hot coals. Coat the inside of a large Dutch oven with olive oil; set aside. Place melted butter in a shallow bowl; mix together cheese and seasonings in another shallow bowl. Dip chicken into butter; coat with cheese mixture. Arrange chicken in Dutch oven; set on 10 to 12 hot coals in campfire. Add lid; arrange another 10 to 12 coals on lid. Cook for 45 to 50 minutes, until golden and chicken juices run clear, adding more hot coals as needed. May also bake, covered, at 350 degrees for 35 to 40 minutes. Makes 4 to 6 servings.

Whip up a simple rustic centerpiece... fill an old-fashioned colander with colorful apples and pears. They're perfect for snacking too.

Harvest
for Sharing

Gigi's Thanksgiving Turkey & Gravy

Glenda Tolbert
Moore, SC

I learned this recipe from my mom and everyone likes it. Some people save the giblets to cook in the gravy, I don't. If your turkey is larger than 12 pounds, check the package for the baking time.

10 to 12-lb. turkey, thawed
    if frozen
salt to taste

1 onion, peeled
1 T. salt

Remove giblet packages from turkey; clean both cavities. Pat turkey dry; sprinkle well with salt, inside and out. Place turkey in a large bowl or pan. Cover with saran wrap and then aluminum foil; refrigerate overnight. The next morning, uncover turkey; place in a roaster with a lid. Place onion in cavity. Add 3 inches water to pan around turkey. Add one tablespoon salt to water; cover with lid. Bake at 325 degrees for 3 hours. Uncover; bake an additional 30 minutes, or until a meat thermometer reads 165 degrees. Remove turkey to a platter and cover loosely; reserve 2 cups broth from pan for gravy. Slice turkey; serve with gravy. Serves 8 to 10.

Gravy:

2 c. reserved turkey broth
2 T. all-purpose flour

1/4 c. milk

Heat broth in a saucepan over medium heat. Mix flour and milk in a cup; gradually add to broth. Cook and stir until thickened.

Handprint turkeys are a Thanksgiving classic! Turn the kids loose, drawing turkeys around their hands on a stack of folded large index cards. Add the names of family & friends joining you for the big day...they'll be charmed.

Chicken with Dijon-Cranberry Sauce

Ellen Meade
Las Vegas, NV

I wanted a recipe that was reminiscent of Thanksgiving but could be enjoyed at other times of the year. I think I succeeded! Serve over cooked rice, noodles or potatoes.

2 boneless, skinless chicken
   breasts
1/2 c. all-purpose flour
2 T. butter
2 T. extra-virgin olive oil
1-1/2 c. water

1/2 c. low-sodium chicken
   or vegetable broth
1/2 c. dried cranberries
salt and pepper to taste
2 T. Dijon mustard

Slice each chicken breast into 2 fillets; coat fillets with flour. In a skillet over medium heat, melt butter with olive oil. Add chicken breasts to skillet; sauté on both sides until lightly golden. Remove chicken to a plate. To drippings in pan, add water, broth, cranberries, salt and pepper. Gently sauté over medium-low heat for 2 to 3 minutes. Add mustard; stir well. Return chicken to pan; turn to coat with sauce. Cover and sauté over low heat for 2 to 3 minutes, until chicken is cooked through. Stir in a little more water, if needed. Serves 4.

I can see the woods in their autumn dress, the oaks purple, the hickories washed with gold, the maples and the sumacs luminous with crimson fires.

–Mark Twain

Harvest
for Sharing

Slow-Cooker Pot Roast

Jennie Gist
Gooseberry Patch

For old-fashioned comfort, you can't beat a pot roast! I like to prep the veggies the night before and tuck them in the fridge. In the morning, I just fill up the crock, set and forget.

1 T. cornstarch
2 T. cold water
6 to 8 carrots, peeled and cut
   into thirds
2 onions, cut into wedges

3 to 3-1/2 lb. beef chuck roast
1 t. seasoned salt
1/2 t. pepper
garlic powder to taste
2 T. Worcestershire sauce

In a 5-quart slow cooker, stir together cornstarch and cold water until smooth. Add carrots and onions; toss. Sprinkle roast with seasonings. Place roast on top of vegetables; drizzle with Worcestershire sauce. Cover and cook on low setting for 6 to 8 hours, or on high setting for 4 to 5 hours. Transfer roast to a platter; slice or shred. Serve roast with vegetables and juices from slow cooker. Serves 6 to 8.

Take it easy when planning holiday dinners...stick to familiar, tried & true recipes! Guests are often just as happy with simple comfort foods as with the most elegant gourmet meal.

Feasts for Family & Friends

Sassy Salsa Chicken

Suzanne Matlosz
Mesa, AZ

This slow-cooker recipe was one of my dad's favorite meals. He has been gone a few years now and whenever I make this, I think of him. We would mix it up and use different salsas each time we made it. I like to use mango salsa. The chicken will break up as it cooks.

16-oz. pkg. baby carrots
2-1/2 lb. pkg. boneless, skinless
   chicken breasts, partially
   thawed

16-oz. jar chunky mango salsa
   or other favorite salsa
3 to 6 c. cooked rice
6 8-inch flour tortillas

Spread carrots in a 5-quart slow cooker. Place chicken pieces on top of carrots; spoon salsa over chicken. Cover and cook on low setting for 6 to 8 hours. Stir mixture halfway through cooking time to coat chicken with salsa. To serve, spread cooked rice in a serving bowl; transfer chicken and carrots to bowl. Spoon salsa (with or without the liquid) over chicken. Serve with a folded tortilla on side of each plate. Makes 6 servings.

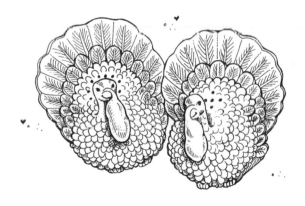

There's always room for one more at the harvest table. Why not invite a neighbor or a college student who might be spending the holiday alone to share your Thanksgiving feast?

Harvest
for Sharing

Cabbage & Brats Skillet

Courtney Stultz
Weir, KS

We love hearty, wholesome meals that are quick to prepare.
This meal is easy and is loaded with flavor! We like to use
bison brats. Great for busy weeknights.

2 T. coconut or canola oil
2 to 3 potatoes, peeled and cubed
1 c. cabbage, cubed
1/4 c. onion, cubed
3 bratwurst sausages, cubed
   or sliced
1/2 t. garlic, minced

1/2 t. dried thyme
1/2 t. paprika
1/4 t. caraway seed
1 t. sea salt
1/2 t. pepper
Optional: favorite mustard

Heat oil in a large skillet over medium heat; add potatoes, cabbage and onion. Sauté over medium heat for about 15 minutes, until potatoes are cooked through and beginning to turn golden. Add sausages, garlic and seasonings; cook for an additional 10 minutes. Top with a drizzle of mustard, if desired. Makes 4 servings.

Host an Oktoberfest party for family & friends. Toss some brats
on the grill to serve in hard rolls...don't forget the spicy mustard!
Round out the menu with potato salad, homemade applesauce
and German chocolate cake for dessert. Set a festive mood
with polka music...sure to be wunderbar!

Feasts for
Family & Friends

Ann's Baked Ham

Patricia Thomas
Cataula, GA

For nearly 50 years, my family has requested that I cook this ham for Thanksgiving and Christmas. The secret to this great-tasting baked ham is the time spent baking and basting it.

15 to 20-lb. fully cooked
   cured ham
20-oz. can pineapple slices,
   drained and juice reserved

12-oz. jar maraschino cherries,
   drained and juice reserved

Pat ham dry and place in a roasting pan. Using wooden toothpicks, fasten pineapple slices all over ham, beginning at the top. Fasten 2 cherries in the center of each pineapple slice. Spoon reserved pineapple and cherry juices all over ham. Cover with aluminum foil. Bake at 350 degrees for 3-1/2 to 4 hours, spooning pan juices over pineapple slices twice every 30 minutes. Ham is done when skin is golden and a meat thermometer inserted in thickest part reads 145 degrees. Remove ham to a platter; let stand for 10 to 15 minutes and slice. Serves 20 to 25.

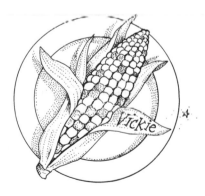

Such clever placecards! Pull back the husks on ears of mini Indian corn and use a bronze or gold paint pen to write the name of each guest along the husks.

Harvest
for Sharing

Cheese-Filled Manicotti

Kathleen Sturm
Corona, CA

This is such an easy and delicious dinner to serve your family...you don't need to boil the manicotti shells before filling! Follow these simple directions and you will have perfectly baked manicotti every time. It can even be frozen for a quick meal to keep on hand.

3 c. favorite spaghetti sauce, divided
1 c. water
8-oz. pkg. shredded mozzarella cheese
16-oz. container ricotta cheese
1/2 c. grated Parmesan cheese

2 T. fresh parsley, chopped
1/2 t. salt
1/4 t. pepper
8-oz. pkg. manicotti pasta, uncooked
Optional: additional shredded mozzarella cheese

Combine spaghetti sauce and water in a saucepan over medium heat; bring to a boil. Spread one cup of sauce in a lightly greased 13"x9" baking pan; set aside. In a large bowl, stir together cheeses, parsley, salt and pepper until well combined. Spoon cheese mixture into uncooked manicotti tubes. Arrange manicotti tubes in a single layer over sauce in pan. Spoon remaining hot sauce over manicotti, covering as well as possible. Cover with aluminum foil. Bake at 400 degrees for 40 minutes. Remove foil; top with extra mozzarella cheese, if desired. Bake, uncovered, an additional 10 minutes, or until bubbly and cheese is melted. Makes 6 to 8 servings.

To make ahead and freeze: prepare and bake as directed; let cool for 30 minutes. Cover tightly with plastic wrap, then heavy-duty aluminum foil. Freeze up to 2 months. To serve, thaw overnight in refrigerator; do not bake frozen. Unwrap and re-cover with foil; bake at 350 degrees for one hour.

Shred a block of cheese in a jiffy. Freeze wrapped cheese for 10 to 20 minutes...it will just glide across the grater!

Feasts for Family & Friends

Mama Simpson's Spaghetti Bake

Ashley Rae Sides
South Chesterfield, VT

My mama, Brenda Rae Simpson, was an amazing cook who cooked from the heart. She passed in 2012, and my nanny (who passed in 2022) made this recipe every holiday to keep her memory alive. I want to share with the world a part of Mom's and Nanny's love.

2 lbs. sliced bacon
1 c. yellow onion, chopped
2 16-oz. pkgs. angel hair
    pasta, uncooked
28-oz. can diced tomatoes
29-oz. can tomato sauce
16-oz. pkg. pasteurized process
    cheese, or to taste, cubed
salt and pepper to taste

Cook bacon in a large skillet over medium heat. Drain bacon on paper towels; chop and set aside. In reserved drippings, sauté onion over medium heat until tender. Remove from heat and set aside, drippings included. Meanwhile, in a very large pot, cook pasta according to package directions, just until tender. Drain and transfer to a greased deep 13"x9" baking pan. Add bacon, onion mixture, tomatoes with juice, tomato sauce and cheese; mix well. Season with salt and pepper. Bake, uncovered, at 350 degrees for 15 to 20 minutes, until bubbly and cheese is nicely melted. Makes 10 to 12 servings.

A notepad on the fridge is handy for a running grocery list...no more running to the store at the last minute before starting dinner!

Harvest
for Sharing

Shrimp & Grits

Jacki Smith
Fayetteville, NC

Every year for Thanksgiving, my dad would cook shrimp as an appetizer for our meal. I would always use the leftover shrimp to make Shrimp & Grits the next day. It's something we all look forward to, after all the turkey & dressing! Add a crisp tossed salad and some hot garlic bread for a wonderful dinner.

1 c. long-cooking grits, uncooked
2 c. shredded Cheddar cheese
1 c. shredded white Cheddar
    cheese
3/4 lb. sliced bacon, diced

2 c. sliced mushrooms
1 bunch green onions, chopped
1 lemon, halved
1 T. hot pepper sauce, or to taste
1 lb. cooked shrimp, peeled

In a large saucepan, cook grits according to package directions. Add cheeses to cooked grits and stir well. Meanwhile, cook bacon in a large skillet over medium heat until crisp. Transfer bacon to paper towels, reserving drippings. Add mushrooms and onions to reserved drippings; cook until tender. Squeeze juice from lemon halves over mushroom mixture; drizzle with hot sauce. Add cooked shrimp to mushroom mixture; cook and stir until warmed through. Crumble bacon and return to skillet. Serve shrimp and mushroom mixture ladled over the cheese grits. Makes 6 servings.

An oh-so-simple harvest decoration...roll out a wheelbarrow and heap it full of large, colorful squash and pumpkins.

Feasts for Family & Friends

Cheesy Tuna Noodle Casserole

Jessica Gladish
Westlake, OH

My mom has been making this recipe for our family since I was a little kid. It began as a quick, cheap and easy dinner for her to make and has become one of our family favorites. I've added just a few of my own tweaks to the recipe.

16-oz. pkg. wide egg noodles, uncooked
10-3/4 oz. can cream of mushroom soup
1-1/2 c. whole milk
2 5-oz. cans chunk light tuna in water, drained
1-1/2 c. mayonnaise
8-oz. pkg. shredded Colby Jack cheese
2 t. salt
1 t. pepper

Cook egg noodles one minute less than package instructions in salted boiling water; drain. Meanwhile, in a saucepan over medium heat, whisk together mushroom soup and milk until well blended. In a large bowl, flake tuna with a fork. Add mayonnaise, cheese and seasonings to tuna; mix until well combined. Add cooked noodles and soup mixture; mix thoroughly. Season with additional salt and pepper, if desired. Transfer to a greased 13"x9" baking pan. Bake, uncovered, at 350 degrees for 30 to 35 minutes, until crisp and golden on top. Makes 8 servings.

Slip children's drawings between two pieces of clear self-adhesive plastic for placemats that are both practical and playful.

Harvest
for Sharing

Turkey Tamale Bake

Karen Davis
Glendale, AZ

By the end of Thanksgiving weekend one year, my family was getting pretty tired of leftover turkey. I found this recipe and swapped out chicken for turkey...problem solved!

8-1/2 oz. pkg. corn muffin mix
14-3/4 oz. can cream-style corn
2 eggs, beaten
1/2 c. milk
1 t. chili powder

1/2 t. ground cumin
8-oz. pkg. shredded Mexican-
 blend cheese, divided
3 c. roast turkey, shredded
10-oz. can red enchilada sauce

In a large bowl, combine dry muffin mix, corn, eggs, milk, seasonings and one cup cheese. Mix well; spread in a lightly greased 13"x9" baking pan. Bake, uncovered, at 400 degrees for 20 minutes. Meanwhile, in another bowl, toss turkey with enchilada sauce. Spoon turkey mixture over baked cornbread; top with remaining cheese. Bake, uncovered, at 400 degrees for an 20 additional minutes. Allow to cool for 5 minutes; cut into squares. Makes 6 to 8 servings.

The day after Thanksgiving, host your own chef competition! It's fun to see who can turn yesterday's juicy turkey or savory stuffing into an exciting new recipe...you may just create a brand-new family favorite.

Feasts for Family & Friends

Slow-Cooker Italian Chicken & Noodles

Kristy Jensen
Williamsburg, VA

The first time I made this recipe for my family, there wasn't one spoonful left! Made with cream cheese and fresh spinach and basil, it's delicious and easy. Serve with warm bread.

1-1/2 lbs. boneless, skinless chicken breasts
16-oz. bottle zesty Italian salad dressing
1 t. pepper
1/2 c. grated Parmesan cheese, divided

8-oz. pkg. cream cheese, softened
2 c. fresh spinach, torn
1/2 c. fresh basil, chopped
16-oz. pkg. bowtie pasta, uncooked

Place chicken breasts in a 5-quart slow cooker coated with non-stick vegetable spray. Pour salad dressing over chicken; top with pepper and half of Parmesan cheese. Place block of cream cheese on top. Cover and cook on low setting for 6 to 8 hours, or on high setting for 4 hours. Shred chicken with 2 forks and mix everything together well. Add spinach, basil and remaining Parmesan cheese to crock. Cover and cook for 20 minutes more. Meanwhile, cook pasta according to package directions; drain. Stir chicken mixture in slow cooker; add pasta to crock. Stir gently and serve. Makes 6 servings.

Make some hot garlic bread...yum! Cut a loaf of Italian bread in half lengthwise. Blend 1/2 cup softened butter with 2 minced garlic cloves, one tablespoon chopped fresh parsley and 1/4 cup grated Parmesan cheese. Spread over cut sides of bread and broil 2 to 3 minutes, until golden and bubbly. Slice and serve.

Taco Tuesday Chicken Pasta Bake

Theresa Eldridge
Festus, MO

We love Taco Tuesdays! But with four kids, cooking can be a real time challenge. This recipe is delicious and easy whenever you need something you can prep ahead of time. Serve with a side salad, chips and salsa...fast, easy and delicious! Rotisserie chicken works great, or in a pinch, you can use two large cans of chunk chicken, drained and rinsed.

16-oz. pkg. spaghetti, uncooked
2 c. cooked chicken, diced
2 10-3/4 oz. cans cream of
   chicken soup
1 c. favorite salsa

1 c. sour cream
1 T. taco seasoning mix,
   or to taste
2 to 2-1/2 c. finely shredded
   Colby Jack cheese, divided

Cook spaghetti according to package directions; drain and transfer to a large bowl. Add chicken, chicken soup, salsa, sour cream, taco seasoning and 1-1/2 cups cheese. Stir to combine well; spread evenly in a 13"x9" baking pan sprayed with non-stick vegetable spray. Top with desired amount of remaining cheese. Cover with non-stick aluminum foil, or spray foil and cover pan sprayed-side down. Bake at 350 degrees for 25 minutes, or until cheese begins to turn bubbly and lightly golden. Makes 6 servings.

A muffin tin is useful when you're serving tacos or enchiladas with lots of tasty toppings. Fill up the sections with shredded cheese, guacamole, diced tomatoes and sour cream... let everyone mix & match their favorites!

Feasts for Family & Friends

Corn Chip Bake

Nancy Kailihiwa
Wheatland, CA

When my kids were little, they objected to the word "casserole" so I changed it to "bake." Even though they are grown men now, we still call this a bake. Serve with your favorite taco sides.

1 lb. lean ground beef or
    ground turkey
1/2 c. onion, diced
1-oz. pkg. taco seasoning mix
10-oz. can enchilada sauce

15-oz. can ranch-style beans
3/4 c. favorite salsa
9-oz. pkg. corn chips, divided
3 c. shredded sharp Cheddar
    cheese, divided

In a skillet over medium heat, brown beef or turkey with onion; drain. Stir in taco seasoning, enchilada sauce, undrained beans and salsa. Mix well. Simmer for an additional 5 minutes, or until thickened. Spread 3/4 of corn chips evenly in a greased 13"x9" baking pan; top with half of cheese. Top with beef mixture; add remaining cheese. Bake, uncovered, at 350 degrees for 25 minutes. Remove from oven; top with remaining corn chips. Return to oven for another 5 minutes. Makes 6 to 8 servings.

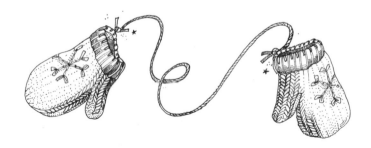

At Thanksgiving, bundle everyone up in their merriest mittens, hats and coats and go outdoors! While everyone's home, it's the perfect time to take photos for this year's Christmas cards.

Harvest
for Sharing

Oven Bar-B-Que Chicken

Nancy Lambert
West Jordan, UT

This is a delicious and versatile recipe. Great for tailgate get-togethers or a lazy-day picnic lunch. We love it served either hot or cold!

3 lbs. chicken thighs, drumsticks
    and/or breasts
salt and pepper to taste
1/2 c. onion, chopped
2 stalks celery, diced
1 T. butter, melted

1 c. catsup
1 c. water
1/4 c. brown sugar, packed
2 T. Worcestershire sauce
2 T. vinegar

Arrange chicken pieces in a greased 13"x9" baking pan. Season with salt and pepper; set aside. In a skillet over medium heat, cook onion and celery in butter until tender. Stir in remaining ingredients; simmer until slightly thickened. Spoon sauce over chicken. Bake, uncovered, at 350 degrees for about one hour, until chicken juices run clear, basting occasionally with sauce in pan. Serve chicken with remaining sauce. Makes 4 to 5 servings.

Start a family tradition. Before dinner, take time to hold hands and ask everyone at the table to share what they're thankful for... some of the sweetest memories will be made.

Feasts for
Family & Friends

Family-Favorite Beer Sausage

Annette Ceravolo
Hoover, AL

This recipe has been in my family for many years. It's easy to make and tastes so good. I like to serve it with steamed vegetables and warm Italian bread. It freezes well, if there are any leftovers.

1 lb. hot Italian pork sausage
   links, cut into 1/2-inch pieces
1 lb. mild Italian pork sausage
   links, cut into 1/2-inch pieces
1 c. onion, minced

1 c. light-colored regular or
   non-alcoholic beer
1 T. fresh parsley, finely chopped
1/2 t. hot pepper sauce

Cook sausage in a large skillet over medium-high heat until lightly browned; drain. Add onion and cook for 5 to 6 minutes. Reduce heat to low; slowly stir in beer, parsley and pepper sauce. Simmer for 10 minutes, stirring every 3 minutes. Spread onto a serving platter. Makes 8 to 10 servings.

Smoked Sausage & Bowties

Leanne Wheless
Borger, TX

I'm forever trying to think of new ways to cook smoked sausage. My husband loves the ones made with cheese inside.

2 t. butter
14-oz. pkg. smoked pork
   sausage with cheese,
   thinly sliced
1 T. dried, minced onions
1 t. dried, minced garlic
2 c. chicken broth

1/2 c. milk
10-oz. can Italian-seasoned
   diced tomatoes
8-oz. pkg. mini bowtie pasta,
   uncooked
1 c. shredded Italian-blend
   cheese, divided

Melt butter in a skillet over medium heat. Brown sausage with onions and garlic. Meanwhile, in a saucepan over medium-high heat, combine chicken broth, milk and tomatoes with juice. Bring to a boil; stir in pasta. Reduce heat to medium-low; cover and simmer until pasta is tender. Turn off heat. Stir in sausage mixture and 3/4 cup cheese; let stand for 5 minutes. Serve in bowls, topped with remaining cheese. Serves 4 to 6.

Harvest
for Sharing

Slow-Cooker Spiced Cider Pork Loin

Shandy Showers
DeKalb, IL

I love the smell of fall! Few things are more comforting than wonderful fall smells like spiced cider, coming from the heart of the home. This slow-cooker recipe is just right for a cozy dinner. Be sure to use a nice rich cider, not apple juice. For an easy and delicious lunch the next day, double the recipe and make shredded pork & apple butter sandwiches on sweet Hawaiian rolls.

2 c. carrots, peeled and sliced
2 Granny Smith apples, cored
   and cut into wedges
1-1/2 lb. pork tenderloin
2 t. garlic, minced
3 c. apple cider
1/2 t. nutmeg

1/4 t. cinnamon
1/4 t. ground cloves
1/4 t. salt
1/8 t. pepper
3/4 c. apple butter
seasoned salt to taste
1 T. butter, diced

In a 4-quart slow cooker, layer carrots, apples, pork loin and garlic; set aside. Combine cider, spices, salt and pepper; spoon over pork loin. Cover and cook on high setting for 5-1/2 hours. Just before serving, heat apple butter in a small saucepan over low heat. Slice the pork and plate with the carrots and apples. Sprinkle seasoned salt over pork; dot carrots with butter. Spoon warm apple butter over pork and serve. Serves 4.

Enjoy the best of the season...take a hayride, visit the apple orchard and pumpkin patch with family & friends. End the day gathered around a bonfire telling stories or singing songs.

Feasts for Family & Friends

Smothered Pork Chops

Betty Cook
Gilmer, TX

*This meal-in-a-pan recipe was born of what I had on hand one day.
My family loved it and it became a regular dish at our table. If you
like more gravy, use 3 cans of soup and 2 cans of evaporated milk.*

3/4 c. all-purpose flour
salt and pepper to taste
6 boneless pork chops, about
   3/4-inch thick
oil for frying
5 to 6 potatoes, peeled and sliced
   1/4-inch thick

2 onions, sliced and separated
   into rings
2 10-3/4 oz. cans cream of
   mushroom soup
5-oz. can evaporated milk

Combine flour, salt and pepper in a deep saucer. Coat both sides of pork
chops in flour mixture. Heat 1/4-inch oil in a large deep skillet over
medium heat. Add pork chops and brown on both sides; drain. Add
potatoes and onions; season with additional salt. Whisk together
mushroom soup and evaporated milk in a bowl; spoon over pork chops
and vegetables. Bring to a boil. Reduce heat to low; simmer until pork
chops are done and potatoes are tender. Makes 6 servings.

A cast-iron skillet is wonderful for cooking up homestyle dinners.
If it hasn't been used in awhile, season it first. Rub it lightly with oil,
bake at 300 degrees for an hour and let it cool completely in the
oven. Now it's ready for many more years of good cooking!

Harvest
for Sharing

Mr. Payne's Beef Enchiladas

Pat Martin
Riverside, CA

Sweet memories from the early 1960s! I learned how to make this unusual version of enchiladas from my teacher Mr. Payne, who led our Christian Education class for teens. Mr. Payne was a military cook and used this recipe to teach us more than just cooking.

1 lb. ground beef
1 onion, diced
1 t. chili powder
1 t. ground cumin
1/2 t. garlic salt
salt and pepper to taste
16-oz. pkg. shredded Cheddar
   cheese, divided

8-oz. pkg. shredded Monterey
   Jack cheese, divided
10-oz. can red or green
   enchilada sauce
corn oil for frying
12 6-inch corn tortillas
2 15-oz. cans chili con carne
   with beans

Brown beef in a skillet over medium heat; drain. Stir in onion, all seasonings, one cup Cheddar cheese and 1/2 cup Monterey Jack cheese; remove from heat. Heat enchilada sauce in a shallow saucepan over medium heat; remove from heat. Heat a small amount of oil in a skillet over medium heat. Lightly fry tortillas on both sides and stack on a plate. To assemble, dip each tortilla into warm enchilada sauce, coating both sides; top with a spoonful of beef mixture and roll up. Place rolled enchiladas in a greased 13"x9" baking pan, seam-side down (typically 10 across and 2 on the side to fill pan). Heat chili in a saucepan over medium heat; spoon over enchiladas. Top with remaining cheeses. Bake, uncovered, at 350 degrees for about 30 minutes, until hot and bubbly. Serves 6, 2 enchiladas each.

A fresh-tasting chopped salad of lettuce and tomatoes is always welcome alongside spicy Mexican dishes. Here's an easy dressing. In a covered jar, combine 3 tablespoons olive oil, 2 tablespoons lime juice, 1/4 teaspoon dry mustard and 1/2 teaspoon salt. Cover and shake until well blended.

Feasts for
Family & Friends

Cafe-Style Pinto Beans

Caroline Frazier
Rocklin, CA

Old cafes are my favorite places to stop and eat on traveling journeys. This slow-cooker creation came after tasting the beans at one of those small cafes. It's great with iron skillet cornbread!

32-oz. pkg. dried pinto beans,
   rinsed and sorted
1 lb. sliced bacon, chopped
1 onion, sliced
1-oz. pkg. Tex-Mex-style chili
   seasoning mix

1/2 c. brown sugar, packed
1/4 c. pickled jalapeño slices,
   drained and 1 T. liquid
   reserved
1 smoked ham hock
2 T. olive or canola oil

Cover beans with water in a large bowl; soak for 8 hours or overnight. Drain beans; place in a 6-quart slow cooker. Add remaining ingredients except oil; stir. Add enough water to fill crock to one inch over beans. Stir in oil. Cover and cook on low setting for 8 hours. Makes 16 servings.

Back-to-School
Baby Back Ribs

Mary Thomason-Smith
Bloomington, IN

Weekends after the kids go back to school are a special time to reconnect as a family. These ribs combine the best of smoky flavors with the ease of slow cooking, for melt-in-your-mouth pork ribs that have everyone coming back for more. Serve with cornbread and coleslaw.

1/2 c. brown sugar, packed
1 T. smoked paprika
1 T. garlic powder
2 t. chili powder

2 t. salt
1/2 t. pepper
2-lb. rack pork baby back ribs
3 T. favorite barbecue sauce

Combine all ingredients except ribs and barbecue sauce; coat both sides of ribs with mixture. Place ribs in a slow cooker, wide-end down, standing with bone side against the cooker. Drizzle with sauce. Cover and cook on low setting for 10 to 12 hours. For a smoky finish, remove ribs to a baking sheet; bake at 400 degrees for 10 minutes. Serves 4.

Harvest
for Sharing

Lemony Fish Roll-Ups

Barb Bargdill
Gooseberry Patch

*A light meal-in-one that we enjoy. Just add a basket of
hot rolls and some lemon wedges to squeeze over the fish.*

1/3 c. lemon juice
1/3 c. butter, melted
2 t. salt
1/4 t. pepper
10-oz. pkg. frozen chopped
   broccoli, thawed and
   well drained

1 c. cooked rice
1 c. shredded Cheddar cheese
2 lbs. cod or flounder fillets,
   thawed if frozen
paprika to taste

In a small bowl, combine lemon juice, melted butter, salt and pepper;
set aside. Transfer 1/4 cup lemon mixture to another bowl. Add broccoli,
rice and cheese; mix well. Divide rice mixture among fish fillets; roll up.
Arrange seam-side down in a greased 13"x9" baking pan. Spoon
remaining lemon mixture over roll-ups. Bake, uncovered, at 375 degrees
for 15 to 25 minutes, until fish flakes easily with a fork. Sprinkle with
paprika and serve. Serves 4 to 6.

As I cleaned my kitchen after a long day of
canning, I began to hear a familiar sound
that made me smile. It was the popping
sound of lids sealing to quart-sized Mason
jars full of green beans. I was immediately
reminded of growing up living next-door to
Granny and Pops, my grandparents. Pops
always planted a big garden, and when the green beans were ready
he'd place baskets of green beans on the back porch. The ladies from
our family would gather for what Granny called a "Bean Stringing
Party." Then, later that night when everyone else was gone, and Pops
was fast asleep, Granny and I would be the last two workers left.
There we would stand in the basement, listening for lids to pop on
our Mason jars full of green beans. It was so exciting to me! I still
love to hear that popping sound of canning jar lids sealing.

–Monica Britt, Fairdale, WV

Feasts for
Family & Friends

Mother's Shrimp Puff

Lisa Cunningham
Boothbay, ME

My mother has made this for years. It's delicious and super-simple...
so comforting on a cool night. There are never any leftovers! Enjoy
with simmered green beans or steamed broccoli.

6 eggs
3 c. whole milk
3/4 t. dry mustard
1/2 t. pepper
2 c. cooked shrimp, peeled

8-oz. pkg. shredded
   Cheddar cheese
9 slices white bread, crusts
   removed and cubed

Beat eggs in a large bowl; whisk in milk and seasonings. Stir in shrimp, cheese and bread cubes; spoon into a lightly greased 13"x9" baking pan. Bake, uncovered, at 325 degrees for one hour, or until a knife tip inserted in the center comes out clean. Serves 6.

Shrimp Noodle Bowls

Jill Burton
Gooseberry Patch

A quick & easy meal to share with a friend.

4 c. water
2 3-oz. pkgs. soy sauce-
   flavored ramen noodle
   soup mix, divided
2 green onions, chopped
2 T. fresh cilantro or parsley,
   chopped

1 c. fresh snow peas, trimmed
12 uncooked medium shrimp,
   peeled and cleaned
1/2 c. Napa cabbage, finely
   shredded
2 to 4 T. chopped peanuts

In a saucepan over medium heat, combine water, ramen flavor packets, green onions and cilantro or parsley. Bring to a boil. Add ramen noodles and snow peas; simmer for one minute. Stir in shrimp; simmer for 2 minutes, or until noodles are done. Divide between 2 soup plates; top with cabbage and peanuts. Serves 2.

Harvest
for Sharing

Milwaukee Pork Stew

Shelley Turner
Boise, ID

When family & friends gather for dinner, I love to serve them this hearty stew, ladled over scoops over mashed potatoes. Add some chunky applesauce and rye rolls on the side for a wonderful meal.

3 to 4 lbs. boneless pork
   shoulder roast, cubed
1/3 c. all-purpose flour
1-1/2 t. salt
1/4 t. pepper
2 T. oil
4 onions, thickly sliced
1 clove garlic, pressed

14-1/2 oz. can chicken broth
12-oz. bottle favorite regular or
   non-alcoholic beer
2 T. red wine vinegar
1 t. brown sugar, packed
1 t. caraway seed
1 bay leaf

Place pork cubes in one-gallon plastic zipping bag; set aside. In a cup, mix together flour, salt and pepper; add to bag. Turn bag to coat pork cubes well. Heat oil in a Dutch oven over medium-high heat; cook pork cubes on all sides until golden. Add onions and garlic; cook until onions are soft, stirring occasionally. Stir in remaining ingredients. Bring to a boil; reduce heat to medium-low. Cover and simmer for one hour, until pork is very tender, stirring occasionally. Discard bay leaf and serve. Serves 6 to 8.

Whip up a simple rustic centerpiece...fill an old-fashioned colander with colorful apples. They're perfect for snacking on too!

Feasts for
Family & Friends

Slow-Cooker Bourbon Chicken

Angela Lengacher
Montgomery, IN

*Easy and delicious! If you like, stir in a little cornstarch near
the end of cooking time to thicken up the sauce a little.*

2-1/2 lbs. boneless, skinless
    chicken thighs, fat trimmed
salt and pepper to taste
3/4 c. soy sauce, divided
3/4 c. honey
1/2 c. catsup

2 T. brown sugar, packed
3 T. oil
1 to 2 cloves garlic, pressed
1/2 t. red pepper flakes
cooked rice

Pat chicken thighs dry with paper towels. Season with salt and pepper;
arrange in a 5-quart slow cooker. Spoon 1/4 cup soy sauce over
chicken. Cover and cook on low setting for 3 to 4 hours, or on high
setting for 2 to 3 hours, until chicken is tender. Remove chicken to a
plate; cool. Cube chicken and return to slow cooker. In a bowl, whisk
together remaining soy sauce and other ingredients except rice; spoon
over chicken. Cover and continue cooking on low setting for one to
2 hours. Serve over cooked rice. Makes 6 servings.

Forever on Thanksgiving Day,
The heart will find the pathway home.
–Wilbur D. Nesbit

Harvest
for Sharing

Leftover Turkey Dinner Casserole *Nancy Lanning*
Lancaster, SC

It's always hard to figure out what to do with leftovers, especially at Thanksgiving or Christmas, and this is the perfect casserole! Try it with leftover chicken too.

4 c. cooked stuffing, divided
5 c. roast turkey, shredded
1/4 c. whole-berry cranberry
   sauce
3/4 c. mayonnaise, divided

2 c. mashed potatoes
1-1/2 c. shredded mozzarella
   cheese
Optional: sweetened dried
   cranberries

Spread half of stuffing evenly in a lightly greased 8"x8" baking pan; top with turkey and set aside. In a bowl, combine cranberry sauce and 1/4 cup mayonnaise; spread evenly over turkey. In a large bowl, combine remaining mayonnaise, mashed potatoes and cheese; spread evenly over cranberry sauce. Spread remaining stuffing on top. Bake, uncovered, at 375 degrees for 40 minutes, or until hot and bubbly in the center. Let stand for 10 minutes; garnish with dried cranberries, if desired, and serve. Makes 6 to 8 servings.

Thanksgiving is so family-centered...why not have a post-holiday potluck with friends, the weekend after Turkey Day? Everyone can bring their favorite "leftover" concoctions and relax together.

Feasts for
Family & Friends

Lemon Herbed Chicken

Cami Seager
Ashburn, VA

Easy and so delicious! Serve with cooked noodles or rice.

2 T. oil
4 boneless, skinless chicken
   breasts
10-3/4 oz. can cream of
   celery soup

2 T. lemon juice
1/2 t. paprika
1/4 t. lemon pepper seasoning
1/4 t. dried marjoram

Heat oil in a skillet over medium heat. Cook chicken breasts until golden on both sides; drain. Stir in remaining ingredients; bring to a boil. Reduce heat to low. Cover and simmer for 30 minutes, stirring occasionally, or until chicken is tender. Makes 4 servings.

Provence Pork

Theresa Diulus
Seabrook, TX

This meal is big in flavor, but not on preparation...a great combination in my book! This recipe works well with a boneless turkey breast too. The star is the Herbes de Provence seasoning, which can be found in most supermarkets these days. The smell and taste of the seasoning will have you awaiting the oven timer eagerly.

1 lb. pork tenderloin
1 T. olive oil
1 t. kosher salt

1 T. Herbes de Provence
   seasoning

Pat tenderloin dry; place on a lightly greased sheet pan. Drizzle olive oil over pork loin and rub all over, coating entirely. Sprinkle evenly with seasonings; let stand for 20 minutes. Bake, uncovered, at 350 degrees for 20 to 30 minutes, until a meat thermometer reads 145 degrees. Remove from oven; let stand for 10 minutes before slicing. Serves 6.

Ziti Pizza Casserole

Kathleen Sturm
Corona, CA

I combined favorite flavors from several recipes to devise this dish. It is easy and delicious! Any tube-shaped pasta can be used. It is also good made with using browned and crumbled Italian sausage instead of ground pork. Chopped green peppers are a good addition.

8-oz. pkg. ziti pasta, uncooked
1 lb. lean ground beef
1 lb. ground pork
1 t. garlic powder
1 t. onion powder
24-oz. jar favorite pasta sauce,
   or 3 c. homemade sauce

1 c. shredded Parmesan cheese,
   divided
8-oz. pkg. shredded mozzarella
   cheese
15 to 20 slices pepperoni

Cook pasta according to package directions, just until tender; drain. Meanwhile, cook beef with pork in a large skillet over medium heat until no longer pink; drain and stir in seasonings. Add pasta sauce and 1/2 cup Parmesan cheese; stir to combine. Add cooked pasta to sauce in skillet; mix gently and spoon into a greased 13"x9" baking pan. Sprinkle with mozzarella cheese; arrange pepperoni slices on top and sprinkle with remaining Parmesan cheese. Bake, uncovered, at 350 degrees for 30 to 45 minutes, until hot and bubbly. Makes 6 to 8 servings.

Do you have lots of kids coming over for an after-game party? Make it easy with do-it-yourself mini pizzas or tacos...guests can add their own favorite toppings. Round out the menu with pitchers of soft drinks and a delicious dessert. Simple and fun!

Feasts for
Family & Friends

Slow-Cooker Salisbury Meatballs

Nancy Kailihiwa
Wheatland, CA

This is a dependable worknight go-to meal on our monthly meal rotation. It's easy to toss together in the slow cooker and come home to a hot meal. I like to serve them over wide egg noodles and occasionally over rice. A tossed green salad and hot dinner rolls are excellent additions to this meal.

32-oz. pkg. frozen cooked
    meatballs
1 yellow or white onion, chopped
3 c. beef broth
2 0.87.-oz pkgs. brown gravy
    mix
2 T. catsup

1 T. Worcestershire sauce
1 t. onion powder
1 t. garlic powder
1 t. pepper
2 T. cornstarch
2 T. water

Combine frozen meatballs and onion in a 6-quart slow cooker; set aside. In a large bowl, combine remaining ingredients except cornstarch and water; mix well and spoon over meatball mixture. Cover and cook on low setting for 4 to 6 hours, or on high setting for 2 to 3 hours. When nearly done, mix together cornstarch and water in a cup. Turn slow cooker to high setting; pour cornstarch mixture into slow cooker and stir gently. Cover and cook for 20 more minutes, or until sauce is thickened as desired. Makes 6 to 8 servings.

For a quick & easy side dish, quarter new potatoes and toss
with a little olive oil, salt and pepper. Spread on a baking sheet
and bake at 400 degrees until crisp and golden, 35 to 40 minutes.

Harvest
for Sharing

Enchilada Casserole

Marty Findley
Boyd, TX

This dish is always a hit at church potlucks...it's delicious and makes enough to share. I called this the "Hallelujah Casserole" because everyone in my family of five all liked it! It can be made with either beef or chicken.

2 T. butter
1/4 c. onion, chopped
1/4 c. green pepper, chopped
4-oz. can diced green chiles
10-3/4 oz. can cream of chicken
   or celery soup
8-oz. container sour cream
3-oz. pkg. cream cheese,
   softened

1 c. milk
1/4 t. ground cumin
1 lb. ground beef, browned
   and drained, or 2 c. cooked
   chicken, diced
12 7-inch corn tortillas, each cut
   into 8 wedges
3/4 c. shredded Cheddar or
   Monterey Jack cheese

Melt butter in a skillet over medium heat; cook onion and green pepper until tender. Stir in chiles; remove from heat. In a large bowl, blend soup, sour cream, cream cheese, milk and cumin. Fold in onion mixture and beef or chicken. In a greased 3-quart casserole dish, layer half each of tortilla pieces and beef or chicken mixture. Repeat layering. Cover with aluminum foil and bake at 350 degrees for about 35 minutes. Remove foil; sprinkle with shredded cheese. Return to oven for 5 minutes, or until cheese melts. Serves 10 to 12.

Shine on, shine on, harvest moon up in the sky
–Ruth Etting

Cabbage Casserole

Susan Church
Mio, MI

This casserole is a wonderful comfort meal and easy to prepare. My mom used to make it when I was growing up. Since then, I've become more health-conscious and tweaked the recipe to be a little healthier. I like to serve it with a tossed salad and sometimes whole-grain bread from the bakery.

6 c. cabbage, coarsely shredded
   and divided
3/4 c. onion, chopped
1 to 2 t. oil
1/2 lb. ground beef or soy
   burger crumbles

3/4 t. salt
1/8 t. pepper
10-3/4 oz. can low-sodium
   tomato soup

Spread 3 cups shredded cabbage in a 3-quart casserole dish sprayed with non-stick vegetable spray; set aside. In a skillet over medium heat, sauté onion in oil until softened but not browned. Add beef or soy crumbles; cook and stir until lightly browned. Drain, if needed. Season with salt and pepper. Spread warm beef or soy crumbles over cabbage layer; top with remaining cabbage. Spread tomato soup over top. Cover and bake at 350 degrees for one hour, or until hot and bubbly. Makes 4 servings.

A quick fall craft for kids...hot-glue large acorn caps
onto round magnets for whimsical fridge magnets.

Harvest
for Sharing

Silly String Pie

*Sandy Ward
Anderson, IN*

*Kids seem to like food with fun names, that they can
help you make. This recipe is always a winner!*

8-oz. pkg. spaghetti, uncooked
1 lb. ground beef
1/2 c. onion, chopped
1/4 c. green pepper, chopped
15-oz. jar spaghetti sauce

1/3 c. grated Parmesan cheese
2 eggs, beaten
2 t. butter, melted
1 to 2 c. cottage cheese
1 c. shredded mozzarella cheese

Cook spaghetti according to package directions; drain. Meanwhile,
brown beef with onion and pepper in a skillet over medium heat; drain.
Add sauce to beef mixture and stir well; remove from heat. In a large
bowl, combine cooked spaghetti, Parmesan cheese, eggs and butter; mix
well. Spread in a greased 13"x9" baking pan. Spread beef mixture over
spaghetti layer. Spread desired amount of cottage cheese over sauce; top
with mozzarella cheese. Bake at 350 degrees for 20 minutes, or until
hot and bubbly. Serves 6 to 8.

When my children were young, my husband and I would take them
on our fall trip from Plymouth, Massachusetts to New Hampshire.
We enjoyed seeing the fall leaves changing color. On arrival, we
would go on a hayride, pick apples, make cider on the apple press.
We would buy cinnamon doughnuts and apple cake. Back home,
we made apple pies with the apples we'd bought. This annual
trip is one of my fondest memories, because it's all about family.

–Phyllis McFadden, Plymouth, MA

Tailgate
Get-Togethers

Wonderful Corn Dip

Kathy Neuppert Swanson
Hemet, CA

I love to cook for my husband! This recipe was created with all of his favorite flavors in mind. The creaminess of this dip is so satisfying and mouthwatering. I served it as an appetizer before barbecue dinners to rave reviews. It's just perfect for get-togethers, or as a treat for a hungry husband!

1/4 lb. sliced bacon
14-3/4 oz. can creamed corn
15-1/4 oz. can corn, drained
4-oz. can chopped green chiles
8-oz. pkg. shredded Monterey
    Jack cheese
1/4 c. grated Parmesan cheese
2 T. blue cheese salad dressing

2-1/4 oz. can sliced black olives,
    drained
1/2 red pepper, finely chopped
1/2 onion, finely chopped
8-oz. pkg. cream cheese,
    softened and cubed
1 to 2 T. butter, diced

Cook bacon in a skillet over medium heat until almost crisp. Drain on paper towels; set aside to cool. Meanwhile, in a large bowl, combine remaining ingredients except onion, cream cheese and butter; stir well. Add onion and crumbled bacon; mix well. Spoon into a lightly greased 8"x8" baking pan. Dot with cream cheese and butter. Bake, uncovered, at 350 degrees for 30 to 35 minutes, until hot and bubbly. Serves 4 to 6.

Harvest time is party time! The secret to being a relaxed hostess? Choose foods that can be prepared in advance. At party time, simply pull from the fridge and serve, or pop into a hot oven as needed.

Tailgate
Get-Togethers

Cheesy Pull-Aparts

Jill Ball
Highland, UT

*This is the best game-day food...no football game
would be complete without it!*

1 round loaf sourdough bread
1/2 c. butter, melted
4 cloves garlic, minced

1 c. shredded Cheddar cheese
1/2 c. shredded mozzarella
  cheese

With a serrated knife, cut a criss-cross pattern in top of loaf, slicing it lengthwise, then widthwise. (Do not cut all the way through the bottom.) In a bowl, combine melted butter and garlic. Brush butter mixture inside cuts in loaf, pulling apart each section. Divide cheeses evenly throughout loaf, tucking between sections. Place filled loaf on a length of aluminum foil; wrap foil up and around loaf. Bake at 375 degrees for 15 minutes. Unfold foil; bake another 10 to 15 minutes, until lightly crisp. Remove from oven; serve immediately. Makes 2 dozen.

Serve warm or chilled cider in old-fashioned Mason jars.
Setting the jars inside wire drink carriers makes it
easy to tote them from kitchen to harvest table.

Harvest
for Sharing

Walking Tacos

Vickie
Gooseberry Patch

Easy-to-eat tacos! You might know this as "Tacos in a Bag." Ideal for enjoying at the ballpark, during a football game or family picnic.

1 lb. ground beef
1-1/4 oz. pkg. taco
   seasoning mix
2/3 c. water
8 1-oz. pkgs. corn or
   tortilla chips
2 c. lettuce, shredded

1 to 2 tomatoes, chopped
   and drained
1/2 c. sliced black olives, drained
1 c. shredded Cheddar or
   Mexican-blend cheese
1/2 c. favorite salsa
1/2 c. sour cream

Brown beef in a skillet over medium heat; drain. Stir in taco seasoning and water; bring to a boil. Simmer for 3 to 4 minutes, until thickened; remove from heat. To assemble, gently crush corn chips inside unopened bags; cut each bag open along one side. Spoon equal amounts of all ingredients into each bag. Serve right in the bags with forks. Makes 8 servings.

Invite friends and neighbors to a good old-fashioned block party. Set up picnic tables, arrange lots of chairs in the shade and invite everyone to bring a favorite dish. You're sure to make some wonderful memories together!

Tailgate
Get-Togethers

Fresh Pico de Gallo

Paula Summey
Dallas, GA

One of my favorite recipes that I make on weekends, for cookouts or just whenever I'm craving it. I am always asked to bring this to football parties, potluck or family gatherings. I like to think it's healthy because of all of the yummy fresh ingredients! Serve with tortilla chips, in tacos, on nachos or even as a side dish. Very easy!

4 to 5 roma tomatoes, diced
1/2 bunch fresh cilantro,
   chopped
1 to 2 jalapeño peppers, chopped

1/2 to 3/4 c. red or white
   onion, chopped
juice of 1 lime
sea salt to taste

Add all vegetables to a large bowl; stir until well mixed. Add lime juice and salt; stir again. Cover and chill for 30 minutes before serving. Serves 8.

Bacon-Wrapped Avocados

Laura Martinez
Mount Prospect, IL

This is a recipe that everyone craves and asks for. I like to make them for summer barbecues, but they feel very festive for holiday occasions too!

2 to 3 avocados, halved,
   peeled and pitted
1 lb. sliced bacon

favorite barbecue sauce to taste
Garnish: ranch salad dressing

Slice each avocado into 6 wedges. Wrap each wedge in 1/2 to one bacon slice. Arrange on a parchment paper-lined baking sheet, bacon flap down. Drizzle with barbecue sauce. Bake at 425 degrees for 15 minutes, or until bacon is crisp. Serve with ranch dressing for dipping. Makes 12 to 18 servings.

A grandmother pretends she doesn't know who you are on Halloween.

–Erma Bombeck

Harvest
for Sharing

Parmesan Chicken Brochettes
Mary Jo Klement
La Porte, IN

These appetizers go fast whenever we've made them.
They can be made ahead and frozen before baking.

10 thin wooden skewers
3/4 to 1 lb. boneless, skinless
   chicken breast, cut into
   3/4-inch cubes
1/2 c. butter, melted

1/2 c. fresh bread crumbs
1/2 c. shredded Parmesan cheese
zest of 1 lemon
1 t. dried thyme
3/4 t. seasoned salt

Soak skewers in water for 30 minutes; drain. Arrange 2 to 3 chicken cubes on each skewer. Brush with melted butter and set aside. Combine remaining ingredients in a shallow bowl; roll brochettes in mixture to coat. Place skewers on a non-stick baking sheet. Bake at 400 degrees for 10 minutes, turning after 5 minutes. May also be sautéed in a non-stick skillet for 10 to 15 minutes, turning once. Serve hot. Makes 10 servings.

Fill a vintage teakettle with mulling spices and cinnamon sticks,
then fill with water. Let it gently simmer on the stove
so the sweet fragrance will fill your home.

Tailgate
Get-Togethers

Mississippi Chicken Sandwiches

Emily Doody
Kentwood, MI

This simple and delicious dinner takes only a few simple ingredients added to the slow cooker in the morning. You'll have a warm and tasty dinner ready when you get home! Just add some oven fries or potato chips. Great for party time too!

2 lbs. boneless, skinless
    chicken breasts
1-oz. pkg. reduced-sodium
    brown gravy mix
1-oz. pkg. ranch salad
    dressing mix
1/4 c. banana pepper rings,
    drained and 2 T. juice
    reserved

2 T. butter, sliced
8 hamburger buns, split
Garnish: additional banana
    pepper rings, pickle slices

Place chicken breasts in a 3-quart slow cooker. Sprinkle dry gravy and ranch mixes over chicken. Spoon banana peppers with reserved juice over all; top with butter. Cover and cook on low setting for 5 to 6 hours, until chicken is very tender. Shred chicken and mix back into sauce in slow cooker. To serve, spoon chicken mixture into buns; top with banana peppers and pickles. Makes 8 sandwiches.

Tote your slow cooker to the game-day tailgating party!
Keep hot foods warm and tasty by picking up a power
inverter that will use your car battery to power appliances.

Harvest
for Sharing

Sunday Cheese Sticks

Patricia Taylor
Louisville, KY

Every Sunday night, I would go to my sister's home and enjoy the company of her family watching television. Sometimes we would watch ghost stories, or our favorite older TV shows like "I Love Lucy." It was so cozy in their little den with the fireplace, kids in their snuggly pajamas, and the cats and dogs curled up nearby. My brother-in-law would make the most delicious cheese sticks. I couldn't wait to eat them!

6-1/2 pkg. pizza crust mix
8-oz. pkg. shredded
   mozzarella cheese
8-oz. pkg. shredded mild
   Cheddar cheese

pizza seasoning or dried
   oregano to taste
Optional: warmed pizza sauce

Prepare pizza crust mix according to package directions; spread dough on a 12" round pizza pan. Sprinkle dough generously with cheese; sprinkle with pizza seasoning or oregano. Bake as directed on package, checking every 10 minutes. Remove from oven; allow to cool for 5 minutes and cut into sticks. If desired, serve with warmed pizza sauce for dunking. Serves 5.

There is nothing in the world so irresistibly contagious
as laughter and good humor.
–Charles Dickens

Tailgate
Get-Togethers

Baked Potato Dip

Donna Riggins
Boaz, AL

This is an awesome dip for football games, birthday parties, family gatherings...really, it's good anytime! Serve with chips, carrots and broccoli, or serve as a yummy baked potato topper.

16-oz. container sour cream
1-oz. pkg. ranch salad
   dressing mix
1 lb. sliced bacon, crisply cooked
   and crumbled

8-oz. pkg shredded mild or
   sharp Cheddar cheese

Combine all ingredients in a large bowl; stir until well blended. Cover and chill for one hour before serving. Serves 12.

Tailgate Dip

Olinka Ortiz
El Paso, TX

This simple dip has been a family favorite since I was a child. Every time football was on, I knew Mom would make this dip. And it pairs perfectly with scoop-type corn chips.

24-oz. container small-curd
   cottage cheese
3 to 4 jalapeño peppers, seeded
   and minced

1-1/2 t. garlic powder
2 to 3 t. salt, to taste
1 t. pepper

In a large bowl, combine all ingredients; mix well. Cover and chill until serving. Makes 12 servings.

Hollow out a speckled turban squash and fill with a favorite dip for veggies or chips...a fall twist on a serving bowl!

Harvest
for Sharing

Mushroom Mozzarella Bruschetta

Candace Whitelock
Seaford, DE

This scrumptious warm treat can be adjusted as you like by adding other vegetables and cheeses. It is a very filling appetizer.

1 loaf Italian bread, halved
   lengthwise
10-3/4 oz. can cream of
   mushroom soup
1 c. shredded mozzarella cheese

1 red pepper, diced
2 green onions, chopped
1 T. grated Parmesan cheese
1/4 t. garlic powder
1/4 t. Italian seasoning

Place halves of loaf cut-side up on an ungreased baking sheet. Bake at 400 degrees for 5 minutes, or until loaf is lightly toasted and crusty on the bottom. Remove from oven. Stir together remaining ingredients in a bowl; spread soup mixture over cut sides of loaf. Bake for an additional 5 minutes, or until cheese is melted. Slice and serve warm. Makes 12 servings.

One fall, after visiting our son at a military college in Dahlonega, Georgia, we took off for Helen, Georgia in our convertible to enjoy the brilliant fall colors. We got a giant chocolate chip cookie at Betty's General Store and then headed up Brasstown Bald (highest mountain in Georgia) to enjoy the view. To our surprise, the night before, God had laid down a blanket of snow. We had the best of two worlds...the glorious color of fall leaves in the valley and the bright white of a winter wonderland on the mountain.

–Glenda Tolbert, Moore, SC

Tailgate
Get-Togethers

Sausage & Cream Cheese Wraps

Beckie Apple
Grannis, AR

*These wraps are easy to make and go well with any
game-day fare. We just love them!*

8 10-inch flour tortillas
small amount oil
1 lb. ground pork sausage
3/4 c. onion, chopped
1/2 c. green pepper, chopped

1/2 c. cream cheese, cubed
1 c. shredded Cheddar cheese
4-oz. can diced green chiles
1/4 c. favorite chunky salsa

In a skillet over medium heat, lightly brown and toast tortillas in oil;
set aside. In another skillet over medium heat, cook sausage with onion
and green pepper until fully done, crumbling sausage as much as
possible. Drain; stir in cream cheese and simmer until melted. Add
shredded cheese and stir until melted. Mix in chiles and salsa; remove
from heat. Spoon 1-1/2 heaping tablespoonfuls of sausage mixture onto
each tortilla; roll up tightly and serve. Makes 8 wraps.

Make a party tray of savory bite-size appetizer tarts...
guests will never suspect how easy it is! Bake frozen
mini phyllo shells according to package directions,
then spoon in a favorite creamy dip or spread.

155

Harvest
for Sharing

Garlic Filling Stuffed Bread

Janis Parr
Ontario, Canada

This is a scrumptious hot appetizer that I've served to guests many times. It gets rave reviews from everyone! Serve hot with the reserved bread pieces, crackers or tortilla chips.

1 round bread loaf
2 8-oz. bricks cream cheese,
   room temperature
1 c. shredded Cheddar cheese
1 c. mayonnaise
1/4 c. onion, finely chopped

1 clove garlic, minced
1/2 of a 10-pkg. frozen spinach,
   thawed and drained
1/2 c. bacon, crisply cooked
   and crumbled

Remove just the top piece from the center of loaf. Hollow out the inside of loaf and break into bite-sized pieces; set aside loaf and bread pieces. Combine remaining ingredients in a large bowl; stir well to combine. Spoon cream cheese filling into hollowed-out loaf and wrap loaf well in aluminum foil. Bake at 350 degrees for 45 minutes, or until heated through. Serve with reserved bread pieces. Serves 12 to 15.

No tickets to the big game? Have a tailgate party anyway! Soak up the atmosphere by going to a local high school pep rally or pre-game party. Wear the team colors and cheer them on!

Tailgate
Get-Togethers

Oven-Fried Sesame
Chicken Wings

Paula Marchesi
Auburn, PA

I've been making these tasty wings for the past ten years...they are always the most-requested and the first with an empty plate whenever I serve them! Great during football season.

15 chicken wings
1/2 c. whipping cream
3/4 c. plain dry bread crumbs
2 T. sesame seed

1 t. paprika
1/2 t. salt
1/4 c. butter, melted

Cut wings into 3 sections; discard tips. Place cream in a shallow bowl. In a large resealable plastic zipping bag, combine bread crumbs, sesame seed, paprika and salt. Dip wings into cream and add to bag. Shake bag to coat wings evenly. Spread melted butter in a 13"x9" baking pan. Add wings to pan, turning to coat; arrange in a single layer in pan. Bake, uncovered, at 375 degrees for 40 to 45 minutes, turning wings every 10 minutes, until chicken juices run clear. Makes 2-1/2 dozen.

When it comes to tailgating dippers, serve up lots of variety... hearty crackers, pretzel rods, crisp veggies or slices of thick sourdough or pumpernickel bread. All are just right for creamy dips and spreads.

Harvest
for Sharing

Grandma's Roast Italian Beef

Kimberly Redeker
Savoy, IL

This is a favorite for lunch at Grandma's house. It smells so good, and is great on a crisp, cool day. I never knew how easy this was in a slow cooker until Grandma gave me the recipe. This can be made into sandwiches, and is also tasty on its own.

3 to 4-lb. beef chuck roast
16-oz. jar sliced pepperoncini
   peppers
1.05-oz. pkg. Italian salad
   dressing mix

1 T. seasoned salt
1/3 c. water, or as needed
hard rolls, split, or crusty
   French bread

Place roast in a 5-quart slow cooker; add peppers with juice, seasonings and water, making sure liquid covers roast well. Cover and cook on high setting for 7 to 8 hours, until roast is very tender. Shred roast with 2 forks; stir back into mixture in slow cooker. To serve, spoon beef mixture with peppers into hard rolls or over slices of French bread. Serves 6 to 10.

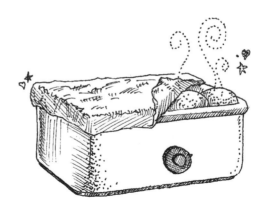

Warm sandwich buns for a crowd...easy! Fill a roaster with buns, cover with heavy-duty aluminum foil and cut several slits in the foil. Top with several dampened paper towels and tightly cover with more foil. Place in a 250-degree oven for 20 minutes. Rolls will be hot and steamy.

Tailgate
Get-Togethers

Hot Spiced Cider

Nancy Lambert
West Jordan, UT

This is wonderful to take to football games. Not only does it make your kitchen smell terrific, it does a fabulous job of warming you up.

1 gal. apple cider
12-oz. can frozen orange
   juice concentrate
12-oz. can frozen lemonade
   concentrate

1/3 c. brown sugar, packed
6 to 8 4-inch cinnamon sticks
12 whole cloves
1/2 whole nutmeg, grated,
   or 1/2 t. ground nutmeg

Combine all ingredients in a large stockpot. Simmer over low heat for 3 to 4 hours, stirring occasionally. Strain and discard spices; serve warm. Makes about 20 servings.

Super Bowl of Beer Cheese

Dian Bentley
Dresden, OH

This creamy, cheesy dip is a perfect hit to serve while watching a football game! Serve with pretzel rods and corn or tortilla chips. You may want to make a double batch!

8-oz. pkg. cream cheese,
   softened
1/2 c. favorite regular or non-
   alcoholic beer

1/2 c. shredded Cheddar cheese
1/2 t. paprika
1/4 t. garlic powder

Combine all ingredients in a large microwave-safe bowl; stir. Microwave on low setting for 30 seconds; stir. Continue to microwave, 10 seconds at a time, until all ingredients are well blended. Stir again and serve warm. Serves 6 to 8.

March pumpkins up a stepladder
for a quick & easy decoration
on the front porch.

Harvest
for Sharing

Stuffed Artie-Chokes

Peter Kay
Naples, FL

This is a quick and delicious way to use canned artichoke hearts. Make sure you get the whole ones, and make sure they are very well drained. They are a bit fragile, but a little careful handling will create this delicious appetizer.

14-oz. can whole artichoke
    hearts in water, well drained
1 egg, beaten
salt and pepper to taste
1 c. all-purpose flour

1 c. Italian-seasoned dry bread
    crumbs
8-oz. pkg. mozzarella cheese
oil for frying

Roll artichokes gently on a paper towel; set aside. In a shallow bowl, whisk egg with salt and pepper. In another shallow bowl, season flour with salt and pepper; spread bread crumbs in another bowl. Cut enough 1/2-inch cubes of mozzarella cheese to equal the number of artichokes. With your thumb, gently open the center of each artichoke; insert a cheese cube inside each. Roll in flour, dip in egg and then roll in bread crumbs. Place all artichokes on a plate; cover and refrigerate for at least 30 minutes. Heat 1/2-inch oil in a skillet over medium heat; add artichokes and gently fry until golden. Drain on paper towels. Serve warm or at room temperature. Serves 4.

Use tiered cake stands for bite-size appetizers...so handy, and they take up less space on the buffet table than setting out several serving platters.

Tailgate
Get-Togethers

Fried Olives

Carmela Tallmeister
Ontario, Canada

This recipe is my take on fried meat cutlets. It's extremely popular at cocktail parties...a perfect addition to a cheese tray.

10-oz. jar jumbo garlic-stuffed
   green olives, drained
3/4 c. all-purpose flour
1 egg, beaten

3/4 c. Italian-seasoned dry bread
   crumbs with cheese
1 c. olive oil for frying

Rinse olives and pat dry. Place flour, beaten egg and bread crumbs in 3 shallow bowls. Dip olives, one at a time, into flour, then egg and then bread crumbs. Heat oil in a small saucepan over medium-high heat. Fry olives, a few at a time, until golden and a crust forms. Serve hot, at room temperature or chilled. Serves 4.

Fried Pickles

Joyce Roebuck
Jacksonville, TX

This is a good appetizer. I buy whole dills and slice them so they aren't so thin. Season with cayenne pepper, if you like.

32-oz. jar whole dill pickles,
   drained
1 egg, beaten
1 c. milk

1 c. all-purpose flour
1 T. cornmeal
canola oil for deep frying

Slice pickles 1/2-inch thick; drain well on paper towels. Whisk together egg and milk in a bowl. Combine flour and cornmeal in a separate bowl. Dip pickles into egg mixture; roll in flour mixture. In a deep saucepan, heat one inch oil to 365 degrees. Add pickles, a few at a time; fry until deeply golden and drain. Makes 3-1/2 cups.

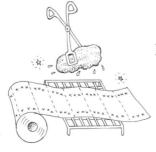

Layer paper towels over a wire rack
set in a baking sheet...perfect for
draining deep-fried treats.

Harvest
for Sharing

Chris's Homemade Salsa

Doreen Knapp
Stanfordville, NY

My friend Chris loved football and graduated from culinary school. He made this recipe for football games and it always was a hit. He went on to open a restaurant. Serve with tortilla chips.

28-oz. can whole tomatoes,
    drained and chopped
1/2 red onion, chopped
1/2 green or red pepper, chopped
1 to 2 jalapeño peppers, chopped
    and seeded
1 T. fresh cilantro, chopped

1 t. cayenne pepper
1 t. red pepper flakes
1 t. salt
1 t. pepper
1/8 t. sugar
1 to 2 T. olive oil
1 to 2 t. red wine vinegar

In a large bowl, combine tomatoes, onion and peppers; stir gently. Add remaining ingredients; mix well. Cover and chill for one to 2 hours before serving. Serves 6.

Serve your favorite salsa with homemade tortilla chips. Simply cut corn tortillas with seasonal cookie cutters. Spritz cut-outs with non-stick vegetable spray and arrange on an ungreased baking sheet. Sprinkle with salt and bake at 350 degrees until crisp, 5 to 10 minutes.

Tailgate
Get-Togethers

Layered Hummus Dip

Cyndy Nene
New Castle, PA

This is my go-to recipe to take to parties and get-togethers when people are trying to eat healthier. It's quick & easy to put together. You can add or subtract any other vegetables as you prefer. Serve with cut veggies, snack crackers or scoop-type tortilla chips.

17-oz. container favorite
   hummus
1-1/2 c. plain Greek yogurt
1 cucumber, diced
1 red pepper, diced
1/4 red onion, diced

1/4 c. Kalamata olives, diced
2 T. olive oil, divided
salt and pepper to taste
4-oz. container crumbled
   feta cheese
2 T. toasted pine nuts

Spread hummus on a shallow rimmed serving tray or platter. Dollop yogurt on top; carefully spread over hummus, leaving a bit of hummus showing on the edges. Set aside. In a small bowl, combine cucumber, pepper, onion, olives and one tablespoon olive oil; mix gently. Season with salt and pepper; spoon over yogurt. Sprinkle with feta cheese and pine nuts. Drizzle lightly with remaining olive oil and serve. Serves 10.

Fright at first sight! Greet guests with spooky decor. Turn a cast-off dollhouse into a tabletop haunted mansion by painting it black...a ghostly greeting for family & friends!

Fall Corn Fritters

Emily Keenan
Choctaw, OK

These fritters are a family favorite and bring back memories of fall football game days. They're served warm with a sweet and spicy Honey Chipotle Dip and are gone before you can blink! They're perfect for tailgating or holiday entertaining.

3/4 c. all-purpose flour
1 t. baking powder
1 T. garlic powder
salt and pepper to taste
1/4 c. shredded Cheddar cheese
1/2 c. milk

1 egg, beaten
2 ears sweet corn, kernels cut off,
 or 15-oz. can corn, drained
1 jalapeño pepper, diced and
 seeded
oil for deep frying

In a bowl, mix flour, baking powder, seasonings and cheese. Add milk and beaten egg; stir until combined. Stir in corn and jalapeño. Add 2 inches of oil to a skillet; heat to 350 degrees over medium-high heat. Working in batches, drop batter into hot oil by tablespoonfuls. Fry for 4 to 5 minutes, flipping halfway through; drain on paper towels. Serve warm fritters with Honey Chipotle Dip. Serves 4.

Honey Chipotle Dip:

1/2 c. mayonnaise
1 T. garlic powder
1 T. lemon juice

1 T. honey
1 t. chipotle chili powder

Blend together all ingredients; cover and chill until serving time.

Bandannas in autumn colors of yellow and gold
make perfect oversized napkins for parties.

Tailgate
Get-Togethers

Game-Day Buffalo Wings

Victoria McGrath
Sarver, PA

A must for game-day gatherings! Serve with plenty of celery sticks and blue cheese dressing. Wear your favorite sports team jersey and enjoy the game and wings!

16 to 18 chicken wings
3/4 c. all-purpose flour
1 T. chili powder
1 T. garlic salt

1 T. cayenne pepper
oil for deep frying
1/2 c. butter
12-oz. bottle buffalo wing sauce

Cut wings into 3 sections; discard tips. Pat dry with paper towels; set aside. Combine flour and seasonings in a large bowl with a lid; add wings. Cover bowl and shake until wings are dredged in flour mixture. Refrigerate, covered, for 4 hours. Heat several inches oil in a deep saucepan over medium-high heat. Add wings, a few at a time; fry until golden and cooked through. Drain; transfer cooked wings to a 13"x9" disposable aluminum pan. Melt butter in a small saucepan; stir in buffalo wing sauce and spoon over wings in pan. Cover with aluminum foil. Bake at 350 degrees for 15 minutes. Serves 4 to 6.

When baking sticky chicken wings or saucy meatballs, be sure to cover the baking pan with heavy-duty aluminum foil, then spray with non-stick vegetable spray. No sticking, no clean-up!

Harvest
for Sharing

Hot Crusty Picnic Loaf

Lynda Hart
Bluffdale, UT

This big Italian sandwich is great for a picnic at the park or to take to the game. It's a meal in itself...just add some chips, olives and drinks. Remember to pack a serrated knife and a small cutting board.

1 flat, round crusty loaf Italian
    bread, halved lengthwise
1 T. olive oil
1/2 t. salt
1/2 t. pepper
4 ripe tomatoes, thinly sliced

7 oz. thinly sliced deli
    mozzarella cheese
5 oz. thinly sliced deli salami
    or other cold cuts
1 T. fresh basil, chopped
1 T. fresh oregano, chopped

With a sharp knife, cut a few slashes in cut sides of both halves of loaf. Brush olive oil on cut sides; sprinkle with salt and pepper. Place both halves on a baking sheet, cut-sides up. Bake at 425 degrees for 5 to 8 minutes. On bottom half of loaf, layer tomatoes, cheese, salami, basil and oregano. Add top half of loaf. Wrap in aluminum foil and a clean kitchen towel; transfer to a picnic basket or cooler with a tight lid. Serves 4.

Every fall we plan a weekend camping trip that is always memorable. We spend all day out in the cool fresh air, exploring nature trails, fishing and riding bikes around the campground. We cook meals around the bonfire, making pizza pies and grilled cheese sandwiches, and finishing with s'mores for dessert. We love our fall camping adventures!

–Melissa Flasck, Rochester Hills, MI

Tailgate
Get-Togethers

Spicy Party Mix

Liz Plotnick-Snay
Gooseberry Patch

A spicy twist on Grandma's party mix that we all know and love.

5 T. butter
1-1/2 t. chili powder
1/2 t. garlic salt
1/2 t. salt
2 c. bite-size crispy corn
  cereal squares

2 c. bite-size crispy rice
  cereal squares
2 c. bite-size crispy wheat
  cereal squares
16-oz. jar dry-roasted peanuts

Melt butter in a large skillet over low heat; stir in seasonings. Add cereals and peanuts. Cook, stirring often, over low heat until all pieces are well coated. Continue cooking and stirring for 10 minutes. Spread cereal mix on paper towels to cool. Store in a covered container. Makes 8 cups.

Pizza Popcorn Spice Mix

Donna Wilson
Maryville, TN

I've had this recipe for popcorn topping a long time now and I just love how it tastes on popcorn. It makes a wonderful gift mix to add to a gift basket, too.

2 T. grated Parmesan cheese
2 T. spaghetti sauce mix

1 t. Italian seasoning
1 t. garlic powder

Mix all ingredients until well blended; store in an airtight container. To use, sprinkle over buttered popcorn. Makes 1/4 cup.

Using recycled jars for food gifts like Pizza Popcorn Snack Mix?
Remove stubborn labels and inked expiration dates with
a swab of rubbing alcohol.

Harvest
for Sharing

Pumpkin Spice Hummus

Eleanor Dionne
Beverly, MA

A great appetizer for fall. It's so simple to make, you may wish to double it! Serve with apple slices and crackers.

15-oz. can chickpeas, drained
1 c. canned pumpkin
1 clove garlic, pressed
Optional: 1 T. water
1/4 t. salt

2 T. lemon juice
2 t. pure maple syrup
2 T. applesauce
1 T. olive oil

In a food processor or blender, combine chickpeas, pumpkin and garlic. Process until smooth; add water if a smoother consistency is desired. Add remaining ingredients; process until combined. Spoon into a container with a tight-fitting lid. Refrigerate until serving time. Makes about 2 cups.

Toffee Caramel Apple Dip

Marsha Baker
Palm Harbor, FL

I love this delicious, fluffy dip that's perfect for fall. Serve with apple slices and gingersnaps...dive in!

8-oz. pkg. cream cheese,
  softened
1/2 c. powdered sugar
8-oz. container frozen whipped
  topping, thawed

1/4 c. plain or chocolate-coated
  toffee bits, divided
1/4 c. caramel topping

In a large bowl, beat cream cheese with an electric mixer on medium speed until smooth. Add powdered sugar; beat until well blended. Reduce speed to low; beat in whipped topping. Stir in half of toffee bits. Spoon dip into a serving bowl; drizzle with caramel sauce and sprinkle with remaining toffee bits. Cover and chill until serving time. Serves 6.

Tailgate
Get-Togethers

Easy Pepper Jelly Appetizer

Mia Rossi
Charlotte, NC

Pepper jelly spooned over a block of cream cheese has been my go-to appetizer for ages, so I was happy to find this simple recipe to make the jelly. So easy and so good! Serve with crackers.

1/2 c. apple jelly
1/2 c. orange marmalade
1 T. jalapeño pepper, chopped
   and seeded

1 T. green onion, chopped
1 t. cider vinegar
8-oz. pkg. cream cheese,
   softened

Combine all ingredients except cream cheese in a saucepan. Cook over low heat, stirring often, until jelly and marmalade are melted and mixture is well blended. Cool; transfer to a covered container and refrigerate for 8 hours. To serve, unwrap cream cheese and place on a serving plate. Spoon jelly over cream cheese and serve. Serves 8.

Create a fall centerpiece in a snap! Hot glue ears of mini Indian corn around a terra cotta pot and set a vase of orange or yellow mums in the center.

Harvest
for Sharing

Maple-Nut Popcorn

Samantha Starks
Madison, WI

Here in Wisconsin, we love our maple syrup! I was tickled to find a new way to enjoy it. I like to make up small bags of the popcorn for party favors, tied with a bow.

10 c. popped popcorn
1 c. butter, cubed
1-1/3 c. sugar
1/4 c. pure maple syrup

1/4 c. light corn syrup
1/2 t. salt
1 t. maple flavoring
1-1/2 c. chopped pecans, toasted

Place popcorn in a large bowl; check for unpopped kernels and set aside. In a heavy saucepan, combine butter, sugar, syrups and salt. Cook and stir over medium heat until mixture reaches the hard-crack stage, or 290 to 310 degrees on a candy thermometer. Remove from heat; stir in maple flavoring and pecans. Quickly pour over popcorn mixture and mix well. Transfer to wax paper-lined baking sheets. Allow to cool and break into clusters. Store in an airtight container. Makes 12 servings.

Fill small paper bags with Maple-Nut Popcorn and tie on handmade tags for sharing with friends. Tuck into a basket alongside apples, mini pumpkins, Indian corn and gourds...such fall fun!

Tailgate
Get-Togethers

Sally's Oven Caramel Corn

Norma Burton
Kuna, ID

This caramel corn has been a hit with family, friends and neighbors for years. My mother-in-law was a good cook and I got this recipe from her, along with many others. From autumn to Christmas, it is in great demand at our house.

16 c. popped popcorn
2 T. butter
2 c. brown sugar, packed
1/2 c. light corn syrup

1 t. salt
1/2 t. baking soda
1 t. vanilla

Divide popped popcorn between 2 large aluminum foil roasting pans. Remove any unpopped kernels and set aside. In a large saucepan over medium heat, combine butter, brown sugar, corn syrup and salt. Bring to a boil; boil for 5 minutes, stirring occasionally. Remove from heat; stir in baking soda and vanilla. Pour over popped popcorn. Bake, uncovered, at 225 degrees for one hour, stirring every 15 minutes. Divide popcorn among several buttered rimmed baking sheets and allow to cool. Break apart; store in a tightly covered container. Makes about 16 cups.

Share chills and thrills with a monster movie night. Make a big batch of popcorn, let the kids each invite a special friend and scatter plump cushions on the floor for extra seating. Sure to be fun for everyone!

Harvest
for Sharing

Artichoke Bruschetta

Lori Rosenberg
Cleveland, OH

This appetizer is a scrumptious marriage of bruschetta and artichoke dip...a winner all the way around! When people taste this, I always hear them say, "Why didn't we think of this earlier?"

6-oz. jar marinated artichoke
   hearts, drained and chopped
1/2 c. shredded Parmesan cheese
1/3 c. onion, minced

1/4 t. garlic powder
5 to 6 T. mayonnaise
16 to 18 thin slices baguette

In a bowl, mix artichokes, Parmesan cheese, onion and garlic powder. Add just enough mayonnaise to make spreadable. Spread mixture on baguette slices; arrange on an ungreased baking sheet. Bake at 350 degrees for 15 to 20 minutes, until topping starts to bubble and turn golden. Serve warm. Serves 6 to 8.

Easy Tailgating Punch

Bethany Scott
Huntsville, AL

So easy to make and carry in...makes enough for a crowd!

12-oz. can frozen citrus-blend
   juice concentrate, thawed
12-oz. can frozen berry-blend
   juice concentrate, thawed

Optional: orange slices
2 2-ltr. bottles ginger ale, chilled
ice cubes

In a one-gallon insulated jug, combine juice concentrates and orange slices, if desired. Cover and chill overnight. At serving time, carefully pour ginger ale into jug; mix gently. Serve over ice cubes. Makes 24 servings.

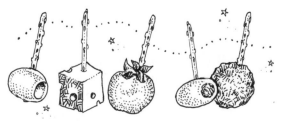

Tailgate
Get-Togethers

Mini Bacon-Ranch Cheese Balls

Ann Farris
Biscoe, AR

This is a different way to serve a cheese ball...fun to add to an appetizer spread!

1-1/2 c. cream cheese, softened
8-oz. pkg. shredded Cheddar
   cheese
1 T. ranch salad dressing mix

1 c. bacon, crisply cooked and
   finely chopped
1 T. fresh parsley, chopped
thin pretzel sticks

In a large bowl, blend cheeses with an electric mixer on medium speed, or by hand. Stir in dressing mix; set aside. In another bowl, combine bacon and parsley. With a melon baller, scoop cheese mixture into small balls; shape with your hands, as needed. Roll balls in bacon mixture; arrange on a tray. Insert a pretzel stick in each cheese ball and serve. Makes 14 servings.

We had six kids in our family and a big yard. Leaf raking was a family project. My dad would get a large tarp and we would rake the leaves into the tarp, jump in them and then drag the tarp back to the woods to empty it. Once, Dad tried to burn the leaves in a huge pile near a telephone pole and accidentally set the pole on fire. The fire department had to come and put out the burning pole and leaves! The next year, we went back to using the tarp...much safer for all!

–Andrea Czarniecki, Northville, MI

Harvest
for Sharing

Autumn Chicken Salad Spread

Carol Hickman
Kingsport, TN

I love Thanksgiving and chicken salad, so I decided to combine my favorites, and it's now our favorite chicken salad! I originally used turkey breast in this recipe, but since chicken breast is more readily available I usually make this as chicken salad. But it's delicious made with turkey, too.

8-oz. pkg. cream cheese,
    softened
1/2 c. mayonnaise
1/2 c. orange marmalade
2 12-1/2 oz. cans shredded
    chicken breast, drained,
    or 2-1/2 c. cooked chicken
    or turkey breast, diced

3 stalks celery, diced
2/3 c. sweetened dried
    cranberries
2/3 c. pecan pieces
1 red apple, cored and diced
28 seedless green grapes, halved
Optional: croissants, sandwich
    bread, crackers

In a large bowl, combine cream cheese, mayonnaise and marmalade; stir until well blended. Add chicken or turkey, celery, cranberries and pecans; stir just until combined. Gently fold in apple and grapes. Cover and chill for several hours before serving on croissants or favorite sandwich bread, or as a dip with crackers. Keeps well in refrigerator for 5 to 7 days. Makes 10 to 12 servings.

Spoon your favorite party spread into a vintage pottery crock...
ideal as a hostess gift. Remember to tie on a spreader too!

Tailgate
Get-Togethers

Apple Cider Refresher

Lynnette Jones
East Flat Rock, NC

Living in Apple Country, we have lots of apple cider in the fall! This is a delicious way to enjoy it.

4 c. apple cider
1 c. pineapple juice
1 c. orange juice

1/4 c. lime juice
Optional: ice cubes or
   crushed ice

Combine all ingredients in a large pitcher; stir well. Cover and chill; serve over ice, or freeze until slushy and serve. Makes 12 servings, 1/2 cup each.

Cranberry Lemonade

Lynda Hart
Bluffdale, UT

This is the perfect fall beverage, and it's a big hit with the kids after school. Keep a big pitcher of it in the fridge!

12-oz. can frozen lemonade
   concentrate, thawed
4 c. cranberry juice
   cocktail, chilled

ice cubes
1-ltr. bottle ginger ale, chilled

Prepare lemonade as label directs in a large pitcher; stir in cranberry juice. Pour over ice in glasses, filling 3/4 full. Top off with ginger ale; stir gently and serve. Makes 12 to 15 servings.

Make your own crystal-clear party ice cubes. Bring a tea kettle of tap water to a boil. Cool to room temperature and pour into ice cube trays, then pop ice cubes into a plastic freezer bag until party time.

Harvest
for Sharing

Easy Queso Dip

Carolyn Deckard
Bedford, IN

*Can't remember where I got this tasty recipe a few years ago.
It goes over great at family get-togethers and it's so
easy. Serve with your favorite tortilla chips.*

1 T. butter
1 jalapeño pepper, finely chopped
   and seeded
1 c. milk
1 T. cornstarch
1 lb. white American cheese,
   cubed

1 t. chili powder
1/2 t. ground cumin
1/4 t. salt
1/4 t. pepper
1/4 t. cayenne pepper

Melt butter in a skillet over medium-high heat. Add jalapeño pepper;
sauté for a few minutes, until tender. Stir in milk and cornstarch; cook
until hot and bubbly. Reduce heat to medium-low. Add cheese cubes;
cook and stir until melted and smooth. Add seasonings; stir until well
blended and serve. Serves 6 to 8.

G-hosting a Halloween buffet? Offer a selection of creepy foods
and beverages, labeled with table tents in your spookiest
handwriting. If you have a specialty that isn't
Halloween-inspired, just give it a spooky new name!

Tailgate
Get-Togethers

Santa Fe Rice

Peg Scott
Turtle Creek, PA

This was the first recipe I taught my daughters in the sixth grade. It can be served hot or cold, as an appetizer with tortilla chips or as a main dish...yum!

1/2 c. onion, diced
1 green pepper, diced
1 to 2 T. oil
1 c. frozen corn

8-oz. jar favorite salsa
2 c. cooked rice
8-oz. pkg. shredded Cheddar
  cheese

In a skillet over medium heat, sauté onion and green pepper in oil until tender. Stir in corn and salsa. Simmer for 10 minutes; drain. Mix in cooked rice; simmer 5 more minutes. Sprinkle with cheese; let stand until melted and serve. Serves 8.

Farmers' Hot Spiced Tomato Juice

Julie Ann Perkins
Anderson, IN

A different way to start off your dinner gatherings! This recipe was tucked away among some very old cookbooks. Both grandmothers clipped & saved recipes, putting them into folders, books & drawers.

46-oz. can tomato juice
6 T. brown sugar, packed
1/2 lemon, sliced

2 4-inch cinnamon sticks
6 whole cloves

Combine all ingredients in a heavy saucepan, enclosing spices in a spice bag if desired. Bring to a boil; simmer for 5 minutes. Stir well; strain and serve hot. Serves 6 to 8.

Going tailgating? Pack a scout-style pocketknife with can opener, corkscrew and other utensils in your picnic kit...so handy!

Harvest
for Sharing

Autumn Snack Mix

Laura Fredlund
Papillion, NE

Fall is my favorite season! I concocted this perfect snack mix to enjoy with my kids while we watch our favorite Halloween movies together.

pumpkin spice doughnut-shaped
    oat cereal
cinnamon bite-size crispy
    cereal squares
caramel corn
salted peanuts

candy-coated chocolates in
    autumn colors
mini pretzel twists
candy pumpkins
candy corn

Combine desired amount of all ingredients in a bowl; toss to mix and serve. Makes as much as you like! One cup of each ingredient will make a big bowlful of 8 cups snack mix.

Pricketts' Pumpkins Farm-Roasted Seeds

Staci Prickett
Montezuma, GA

This recipe can easily be adjusted for the amount of pumpkin seeds you have on hand.

1/4 c. butter, melted
2 t. oil
1 t. Worcestershire sauce
1 t. salt, or to taste

1/2 t. pepper, or to taste
2 c. pumpkin seeds, cleaned
    and patted dry

In a bowl, whisk together butter, oil, Worcestershire sauce, salt and pepper. Add pumpkin seeds; toss until well coated. Spread evenly on an ungreased baking sheet. Bake at 250 degrees for 45 to 50 minutes, tossing seeds every 15 minutes, to desired doneness. Cool; store in a covered container. Makes 2 cups.

Paper cupcake liners come in
all colors...great for serving single
portions of crunchy snacks.

Scrumptious
Cookies &
Desserts

Boo!

Harvest
for Sharing

Oh-So-Good Apple Pie

Pat Beach
Fisherville, KY

My mother-in-law made the best pies ever...they were always a work of art! She loved using her pastry cutter to cut her pie dough into strips for lattice-topped pie crusts. Her apple pies were incredible and I am so glad she shared her recipe with me.

2 9-inch pie crusts, unbaked
6 to 7 tart apples, peeled, cored
   and thinly sliced
3/4 to 1 c. sugar
2 t. all-purpose flour

1/2 to 1 t. cinnamon
1/8 t. nutmeg
1/8 t. salt
2 t. butter, diced
Garnish: additional sugar

Arrange one pie crust in a 9" pie plate; set aside. Add apple slices to a large bowl. Combine sugar, flour, spices and salt; sprinkle over apples and mix well. Spoon apple mixture into pie crust; dot with butter. Cut remaining pie crust into one-inch strips and criss-cross on top; pinch to seal. (May also add crust uncut; cut several vents in crust with a knife tip.) Sprinkle crust with a little extra sugar. Bake at 400 degrees for 50 minutes. Cut into wedges. Makes 8 servings.

Head out to the apple orchard for a day of fun. The kids
will love it, and you'll come home with bushels of
the best-tasting apples for crisps, pies and cobblers!

Scrumptious
Cookies & Desserts

Any Day's a Party Ice Cream Cake

JoAnn Kurtz
Wichita Falls, TX

This cake couldn't be easier. Everyone thinks you worked really hard because it's so good! I make it for birthdays, holidays and any time I want to make people feel special. You can make this dessert days ahead of your party or get-together...a great time-saver for busy days.

15-1/4 oz. pkg. chocolate or
   other cake mix
3 pts. ice cream, all one flavor or
   3 different flavors, softened

3 to 4 c. frozen whipped topping,
   thawed
Garnish: chocolate syrup,
   1 maraschino cherry

Prepare and bake cake mix according to package directions for a 2-layer cake. Cool; cut each layer horizontally to create 4 thin layers. Stack 3 layers on a cake plate, spreading one pint of softened ice cream on each layer; it doesn't have to be perfect. If ice cream is a little firm, spoon it on as evenly as possible. If ice cream gets too soft, place cake in the freezer between layers. Add the remaining layer. Frost cake with whipped topping and drizzle with chocolate syrup. Add a cherry on top and freeze cake until serving time. Let stand at room temperature for about 15 minutes; slice and serve. Makes 16 servings.

I am beginning to learn that it is the sweet and
simple things of life which are the real ones after all.
–Laura Ingalls Wilder

Harvest
for Sharing

Parker's Sneaky Chocolate Chip Cookies

Becky Holsinger
Belpre, OH

My son Parker isn't a fan of very many vegetables. One day, he brought this recipe home from school after his fourth-grade class visited a farmers' market. He just loved these cookies, even though they were made with yams! He begged me to make them and he was right...they are really good. You'd never know they are made with a vegetable!

29-oz. can cut yams, drained
3-1/4 c. all-purpose flour
1-1/2 c. light brown sugar, packed
2 eggs, beaten

1/2 t. salt
1/2 c. butter, softened
2 t. vanilla extract
1 t. baking soda
12-oz. pkg. milk chocolate chips

Place yams in a large bowl and mash. Add flour, brown sugar and eggs; beat well with an electric mixer on medium speed. Add salt and butter; continue beating until fully combined. Beat in vanilla and baking soda. Fold in chocolate chips, using a spatula. Drop dough by rounded teaspoonfuls onto greased baking sheets. Bake at 350 degrees for about 12 minutes. Remove cookies to wire racks; cool completely. Store in an airtight container. Makes 4 dozen.

Fall means back to school, so whip up some tasty treats and greet the kids at the door. Spread out a quilt under the maple tree and spend some quiet time together hearing all about their day.

Scrumptious
Cookies & Desserts

Buttery Spiced Walnut Cookies

Staci Smith
Kissimmee, FL

Holidays are my favorite time of the year! I love the aroma of fresh-baked cookies...the spicy scents are just so comforting. I also like easy, so using a spice cake mix and a pumpkin spice pudding mix brings in all those aromas without buying or measuring spices. Fresh out of the oven, these cookies are a bit soft, but completely cooled, they crisp up, and are perfect for dunking in your favorite warm beverage.

16-1/2 oz. pkg. spice cake mix
3.4-oz. pkg. instant pumpkin
   spice pudding mix
2 eggs, beaten

1 c. chopped walnuts
1 c. butterscotch baking chips
1/2 c. butter, melted

In a large bowl, blend dry cake and pudding mixes; stir in eggs. Add walnuts and butterscotch chips; stir in melted butter. Batter will be thick. Using a 1-1/2 inch cookie scoop, drop dough onto parchment paper-lined baking sheets. With the back of a spatula or your hand, flatten cookies and round out the edges. Bake at 350 degrees for 20 minutes, or just until bottoms are turning golden. Cool on a wire rack. Makes 2 dozen.

Take-home favors in a jiffy! Tie stack of 3 big cookies together
with a length of jute and set in the center of dinner plates
for a sweet surprise.

Harvest
for Sharing

Great-Grandma Walling's Sugar Cookies

Kimberly Redeker
Savoy, IL

I grew up decorating these cookies for all the seasons...Halloween, Christmas, Easter. I can't tell you how much fun I had, and still have. These cookies have a very special taste to them that I never would have guessed. It's the nutmeg! Rolling out cookies with Mom is something I will always remember.

3/4 c. butter
1 c. sugar
2 eggs, beaten
2-3/4 c. all-purpose flour
1 T. baking powder

1/4 t. salt
1/4 t. nutmeg
1/4 c. milk
Garnish: candy sprinkles

In a bowl, beat butter and sugar until light. Stir in eggs and vanilla; set aside. In a separate bowl, sift together flour, baking powder, salt and nutmeg. Add to butter mixture, alternating with milk, mixing well. Cover and refrigerate for about 30 minutes. Divide dough into several portions, returning the remainder to refrigerator. Roll out one portion dough on a floured surface, 1/4-inch thin. Cut with cookie cutters; place on greased baking sheets. Bake at 350 degrees for 11 to 13 minutes; cookies should be soft, not crisp. Cool on wire racks. Frost with Mom's Wedding Cake Frosting; decorate as desired. Makes about 4 dozen.

Mom's Wedding Cake Frosting:

1-1/4 c. shortening
32-oz. pkg. powdered sugar
2/3 c. milk

1-1/2 t. vanilla extract
one to 2 drops butter flavoring

Beat shortening, powdered sugar and milk with an electric mixer on medium speed for 10 minutes. Mix in vanilla and butter flavoring.

For frosting in extra-bright seasonal colors, check a craft store for paste-style food coloring. Just a little goes a long way!

Scrumptious
Cookies & Desserts

Pumpkin Eclair Cake

Cindy Neel
Gooseberry Patch

This creamy dessert is delicious, yet is so easy to make...don't tell your guests!

14.4-oz. pkg. cinnamon graham
   crackers, divided
5.1-oz. pkg. instant vanilla
   pudding mix
2-1/4 c. cold milk
3/4 c. canned pumpkin

1 t. pumpkin pie spice
12-oz. container frozen whipped
   topping, thawed and divided
4-oz. pkg. semi-sweet baking
   chocolate, chopped

Arrange 9 graham crackers in the bottom of an ungreased 13"x9" baking pan, breaking to fit as necessary. Set aside. In a large bowl, whisk together pudding mix and milk for 2 minutes. Stir in pumpkin and spice; let stand for 5 minutes. Add 2 cups whipped topping to pudding; whisk just until blended. Spread half of mixture over crackers in pan; cover with half of remaining crackers. Repeat layering; cover and refrigerate for 3 hours. Combine chocolate and remaining whipped topping in a microwave-safe bowl. Microwave on high for one minute, or until until chocolate is melted. Stir until well blended; spread over dessert. Chill for 15 minutes; cut into squares and serve. Serves 16.

Trick
or
Treat!

Growing up, I always loved Halloween and going trick-or-treating. Two of our neighbor ladies always made scrumptious homemade treats for everyone that included popcorn balls, cookies and fudge. Their house was the one everyone wanted to go to! Many years later, I was reminded of this and wrote them a note to tell them they had made my fondest memory for me as a child. Sadly, they have since passed on, but the memory of them will always be with me and many other children.

–Anita Polizzi, Bakersville, NC

Harvest
for Sharing

Mama's Pumpkin Pie

Maria Chandler
Albuquerque, NM

Handed down from my mother...the only pumpkin pie recipe I ever used. On Thanksgiving Day, it always joined our table with the roast turkey and the lasagna. I grew up in a Italian family, so lasagna was traditional, but so was my mama's pumpkin pie.

2 eggs
15-oz. can pumpkin
3/4 c. brown sugar, packed
1 t. cinnamon

1/2 t. nutmeg
12-oz. can evaporated milk
9-inch pie crust, unbaked

Lightly beat eggs in a large bowl. Stir in remaining ingredients except crust and beat well. Pour into unbaked pie crust. Bake at 425 degrees for 15 minutes; reduce oven temperature to 350 degrees. Bake another 45 to 50 minutes, until a knife tip inserted in the center comes out clean. Cool before slicing; keep refrigerated. Makes 8 servings.

Pear Bundt Cake

Irene Robinson
Cincinnati, OH

This cake is wonderful, moist and easy. Serve plain, or with fruit or ice cream.

15-1/4 oz. can sliced pears in
    light syrup, drained and
    liquid reserved
15-1/2 oz. pkg. white cake mix

2 egg whites
1 whole egg
Garnish: powdered sugar

Chop pears; combine pears and reserved syrup in a large bowl. Add dry cake mix, egg whites and egg. Beat with an electric mixer on low speed for 30 seconds; beat on high speed for 4 minutes. Coat a Bundt® pan with non-stick vegetable spray and dust with flour; add batter. Bake at 350 degrees for 50 to 55 minutes, until a toothpick tests clean. Cool in pan for 10 minutes; turn onto a wire rack and cool. Dust with powdered sugar. Serves 12 to 15.

Scrumptious
Cookies & Desserts

Aunt Edna's Sweet Potato Pies

Alice Joy Randall
Nacogdoches, TX

My Great-Aunt Edna Lee was a wonderful cook. Although she had five children of her own, she was selfless in helping my family as well as many others. She is remembered as someone who loved hosting family holiday dinners.

2 9-inch pie crusts, unbaked
3 c. sweet potatoes, peeled,
   cooked and mashed
1 c. margarine, melted
1-1/2 c. sugar

2 eggs, beaten
14-oz. can sweetened
   condensed milk
1 t. nutmeg

Place each pie crust in a 9" pie plate. Bake at 350 degrees for 15 to 20 minutes, until golden; remove from oven. Meanwhile, combine remaining ingredients in a large bowl; stir until well mixed. Divide filling between baked pie crusts. Bake at 400 degrees for about 30 minutes, until set. Cool completely; cut into wedges. Makes 2 pies; each makes 6 to 8 servings.

Home-baked desserts deserve a dollop of real whipped cream. Using an electric mixer on high speed, beat together 1/2 pint whipping cream with one tablespoon sugar and one teaspoon vanilla until soft peaks form. Scrumptious!

Harvest
for Sharing

School Cafeteria Peanut Butter Bars

Georgia Muth
Penn Valley, CA

A blast from the past! These peanut butter bars take me back to my elementary school cafeteria. I remember the friendly lunch ladies serving these with a smile. Frosting is optional.

2 c. all-purpose flour
2 c. sugar
1 t. baking soda
1 t. salt
2 eggs, beaten

1/2 c. milk
1 t. vanilla extract
1 c. butter, sliced
1 c. creamy peanut butter

In a large bowl, mix together flour, sugar, baking soda and salt; set aside. In a separate bowl, whisk together eggs, milk and vanilla; set aside. In a saucepan over medium heat, melt butter and peanut butter; bring to a boil. Remove from heat; slowly stir in flour mixture. Add egg mixture; stir until well combined. Pour batter into an ungreased rimmed baking sheet; spread evenly to edges. Bake at 400 degrees for about 20 minutes, until a toothpick inserted in the center comes out clean. Cool completely. If desired, spoon warm Peanut Butter Frosting over bars, spreading evenly. Allow frosting to set and cool; cut into bars. Makes 1-1/2 to 2 dozen.

Peanut Butter Frosting:

1/2 c. butter
1/2 c. creamy peanut butter

2 T. milk
4 c. powdered sugar

In a saucepan over medium heat, melt butter and peanut butter; bring to a boil. Stir in milk. Slowly mix in powdered sugar until smooth and well blended.

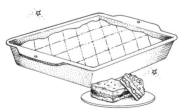

Give bar cookies a fresh new look! Instead of bars or squares, cut cookies into diamond shapes.

Scrumptious
Cookies & Desserts

Best-Ever Brownies

Bethi Hendrickson
Danville, PA

This recipe is a staple at our home. Everyone who eats one always says they are the best...soft and moist.

1 c. butter
2/3 c. regular or dark chocolate
   baking cocoa
4 eggs
2 c. sugar

1 t. vanilla extract
1 c. all-purpose flour
1 t. baking powder
Optional: 1 c. chopped nuts

Melt butter in a small saucepan over medium heat. Add cocoa and mix until smooth; set aside. In a large bowl, beat eggs until light; stir in sugar and vanilla. Add cocoa mixture and beat until well blended. Add flour and baking powder; stir until fluffy. Fold in nuts, if using. Pour batter into a greased 13"x9" baking pan, or an 8"x8" baking pan for thicker brownies. Bake at 350 degrees for 30 minutes. Cut into squares while still hot. Makes one to 1-1/4 dozen.

Be sure to pick up a couple pints of ice cream in pumpkin, cinnamon and other scrumptious seasonal flavors when they're available...they add that special touch to holiday meals!

Caramel Apple Crumble

*Sarah Hente
Saint Charles, MO*

Perfect for autumn! Serve scoops of this scrumptious dessert in bowls, topped with ice cream or whipped cream. Yum!

5 lbs. baking apples, peeled,
    cored and sliced
1-1/2 c. sugar
1/2 t. salt
1 T. cinnamon
1/2 t. nutmeg

1/2 t. ground cloves
1/4 c. caramel baking bits
3 T. chilled butter, diced
1-3/4 c. all-purpose flour
1/2 c. brown sugar, packed
6 T. butter, softened

Place apple slices in a large bowl; set aside. Combine sugar, salt and spices in a small bowl; sprinkle over apples and toss to coat. Let stand for 30 to 45 minutes. Transfer apples to a greased 2-quart casserole dish; sprinkle with caramel bits and dot with diced butter. Bake at 350 degrees for 45 minutes. For topping, combine flour and brown sugar in a bowl. Add softened butter; stir well until mixture resembles crumbs. Sprinkle over hot apple mixture; return to oven for 25 minutes. Makes 6 to 8 servings.

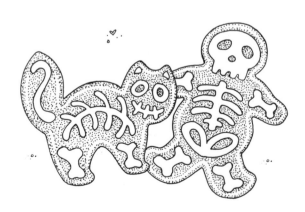

Serve up a batch of skeleton cookies for Halloween! Bake a batch of your favorite gingerbread men. After the cookies are baked and cooled, add "skeletons" using white frosting and a decorator tip. So clever!

Scrumptious
Cookies & Desserts

Baked Indian Pudding

Sharon Velenosi
Costa Mesa, CA

This is a wonderful fall dessert that is well worth the time and effort. If you have an old-fashioned bean pot, it will work very well for this recipe, and makes it a more traditional New England dessert. Serve it warm with whipped cream or vanilla ice cream.

4 c. milk, divided
1/2 c. molasses
1/4 c. cornmeal

1 t. cinnamon
1/2 t. ground ginger
1 t. salt

Add 2 cups milk to a large heavy saucepan over medium-low heat. Heat just to boiling. Meanwhile, in a bowl, mix together remaining ingredients; add to warmed milk and mix well. Cook and stir until mixture is thickened. Pour into a buttered one-quart casserole dish. Cover and bake at 300 degrees for one hour. Pour remaining milk into pudding; stir. Cover and bake an additional 2 hours. Serve warm. Serves 4.

Before I started school, I looked forward to Mom's baking days. She put the extra leaves in the kitchen table and pulled it out into the middle of the room. Newspaper and then wax paper went down, and out came the old blue crock bowl, pie pans and her granddad's sharp-as-a-scalpel knife. I stood transfixed as her hands rolled, shaped and trimmed, making pie after pie that went into our big chest freezer. She always made sure there was dough left over, so I could make what my sister and I called "bumblebees." Now I have my own baking days. My mind always goes back to the kitchen of long ago when Mom made her pies, cakes or equally famous cinnamon rolls. Or when Grandma Ellie came for the summer, and the two of them put up jar after jar of jams and jellies. They handed down not just their recipes, but their love of family and pride in making something special on an ordinary day.

–Susan Ottinger, Mooresville, IN

Harvest
for Sharing

Spiced Apple Butter Bars

Marsha Baker
Palm Harbor, FL

When a friend brought a sample of these delightful treats to my door, I knew I would have to make them again myself. I have used sugar-free apple butter to reduce the amount of sugar and we still thought they were terrific.

16-1/2 oz. pkg. spice or butter
   pecan cake mix
2/3 c. butter, softened
1 egg, beaten
1 c. finely chopped pecans
1 c. apple butter

Line a 9"x9" baking pan with aluminum foil, leaving 2 inches of foil overhanging at 2 opposite sides. Spray foil with non-stick vegetable spray; set aside. In a large bowl, combine dry cake mix, butter and egg. Beat with an electric mixer on low speed for about 2 minutes, just until crumbly. Stir in pecans. Reserve one cup crumb mixture; press remaining mixture into bottom of pan. Spread apple butter over top; crumble reserved crumb mixture over top. Bake at 350 degrees for 30 to 35 minutes, until golden. Set pan on a wire rack; cool completely, about 2 hours. Use foil to lift bars out of pan. Cut and serve, or refrigerate to serve later. Makes 1-1/4 dozen.

Toffee Graham Treats

Joyce Austin
Lacey, WA

Wonderful! Easy to make and requested by family & friends every holiday season.

16 to 18 whole graham crackers,
   broken in half
3/4 c. butter
1 c. brown sugar, packed
1 c. chopped nuts

Lightly grease a 15"x10" jelly-roll pan. Arrange graham cracker squares in pan to cover the bottom; set aside. Melt butter in a saucepan over medium heat; stir in brown sugar. Bring to a boil; boil for 3 minutes, stirring constantly. Spread mixture over graham crackers; sprinkle nuts on top. Bake at 350 degrees for 10 minutes. Cool; break into pieces. Makes 20 servings.

Scrumptious Cookies & Desserts

Maple No-Bake Cookies

Julie Perkins
Anderson, IN

These are always a hit! It would be a good idea to have some copies of the recipe to hand out.

2 c. sugar
1/2 c. margarine
1/2 c. milk
1 c. marshmallow creme

2 t. maple flavoring
5 c. quick-cooking oats, uncooked

Combine sugar, margarine and milk in a large saucepan; bring to a boil over medium heat. Cook at full boil for 2 minutes. Remove from heat; add remaining ingredients and stir until stiff. Drop mixture by teaspoonfuls onto wax paper; allow to cool. Makes about 2 dozen.

Butterscotch Crispy Rice Treats

Lori Gartzke
Fargo, ND

This will take your crispy rice treats to a whole new level!

1/4 c. butter
3.4-oz. pkg. instant butterscotch pudding mix

10-oz. pkg. mini marshmallows
6 c. crispy rice cereal

Melt butter in a large saucepan over medium heat; add dry pudding mix and marshmallows. Cook, stirring constantly, until marshmallows are melted and mixture is smooth. Mix in cereal and coat well. Spoon mixture into a buttered 13"x9" baking pan and press down. Let cool; cut into squares. Makes 1-1/2 dozen.

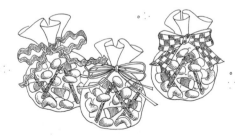

Need a sweet treat for munching in a jiffy? Combine candy corn and salted peanuts in a bowl...yummy!

Happy Birthday Cake

Kathy Neuppert Swanson
Hemet, CA

This cake is incredibly rich and moist...the creamy topping is simple, yet amazing. I made this cake on the first birthday we celebrated with our adopted son, Joseph. He was just five at the time and absolutely loved it! He just turned 20 years old, and I still make it for him every year. Make it for your next birthday party...the recipient will thank you. Or simply serve it after dinner. It's wonderful served with coffee!

15-1/4 oz. pkg. yellow cake mix
3 eggs, beaten
1 c. half-and-half
14-oz. pkg. sweetened
    shredded coconut

12-oz. jar maraschino cherries,
    well drained, chopped and
    patted dry
8-oz. can crushed pineapple

In a large bowl, combine dry cake mix, eggs and half-and-half. Add coconut, cherries and pineapple with juice; mix together well. Batter will be dense. Spread batter in a greased 13"x9" baking pan. Bake at 350 degrees for 30 to 35 minutes, until golden and a toothpick comes out clean. Cool completely; spread with Topping. Refrigerate until chilled. Cake is best served chilled, but may also be served at room temperature. Keep refrigerated. Makes 10 to 12 servings.

Topping:

3 c. whipping cream or milk
5-oz. pkg. instant vanilla
    pudding mix

8-oz. container frozen whipped
    topping, thawed

In a large bowl, combine cream or milk and dry pudding mix. Beat with an electric mixer on low to medium speed for 2 minutes. Gently fold in whipped topping with a spatula. Chill until cake is cooled.

Keep an assortment of colorful candy sprinkles on hand
for dressing up desserts in a jiffy.

Scrumptious
Cookies & Desserts

Easy Monster Cookies

Raksaa Meulenberg
Schenevus, NY

I love these cookies! My aunt and I made them when I was visiting her. They're monstrously good, and the recipe makes a monstrously large batch to share.

3/4 c. butter, softened
1/2 c. sugar
1-1/2 c. brown sugar, packed
4 eggs, beaten
4-1/2 c. quick-cooking oats, uncooked
1 t. vanilla extract

2-1/2 t. baking soda
1/2 t. salt
18-oz. jar creamy peanut butter
12-oz. pkg. semi-sweet chocolate chips
1 c. candy-coated chocolates

In a very large bowl, blend butter and sugars together. Add eggs; beat until fluffy. Add remaining ingredients except chocolate chips and candy-coated chocolates; mix well. Fold in remaining ingredients. Drop dough by heaping teaspoonfuls onto lightly greased baking sheets. Bake at 350 degrees for 8 to 10 minutes, until edges are golden; do not overbake. Cool cookies on wire racks. Makes about 6 dozen.

Stir up some old-fashioned fun this Halloween. Light the house with spooky candlelight and serve homemade popcorn balls, pumpkin cookies and hot cider. Bob for apples and play pin the tail on the black cat...kids of all ages will love it!

Harvest
for Sharing

Pineapple-Cranberry Cake

Nancy Rollag
Kewaskum, WI

This is one of my favorite desserts to make in the fall, when fresh cranberries are available. It's dense, moist and delicious.

3 c. all-purpose flour
2 t. baking soda
1/2 t. salt
1 t. cinnamon
1 t. ground ginger
3 eggs
1-1/2 c. sugar
3/4 c. mayonnaise

20-oz. can crushed pineapple, drained and 1/2 c. juice reserved
12-oz. pkg. fresh cranberries, chopped
1 c. chopped walnuts
1/2 c. raisins
1 T. orange zest

In a bowl, combine flour, baking soda, salt and spices; set aside. Beat eggs in a large bowl; beat in sugar, mayonnaise, pineapple and reserved juice. Gradually add flour mixture to egg mixture, beating until well mixed. Fold in remaining ingredients. Pour batter into a greased and floured 13"x9" baking pan. Bake at 350 degrees for 50 to 55 minutes, until a toothpick inserted in the center comes out clean. Cool completely in pan on a wire rack. Frost with Pineapple Frosting. Cover and refrigerate until frosting is set; cut into squares. Store in refrigerator. Makes 12 to 15 servings.

Pineapple Frosting:

8-oz. pkg. cream cheese, softened
1/2 c. butter, softened
1 c. powdered sugar

1 t. orange zest
8-oz. can crushed pineapple, well drained

Beat together cream cheese and butter. Beat in powdered sugar and orange zest until light and fluffy. Stir in pineapple.

Love fresh cranberries? Stock up when they're available and pop unopened bags in the freezer. They'll keep for months.

Scrumptious Cookies & Desserts

Coconut-Honey Bars

Lisa Barger
Conroe, TX

This old-time recipe is always a hit! It's a great use for that jar of local honey you picked up at a fall festival.

1/2 c. butter, softened
1/2 c. sugar
1/2 c. honey
1 egg, beaten
2/3 c. all-purpose flour
1/2 t. baking powder
1/2 t. baking soda

1/4 t. salt
1 c. quick-cooking oats, uncooked
1 c. flaked coconut
1/2 c. chopped nuts
1 t. vanilla extract

Combine butter, sugar and honey in a large bowl; beat until light and fluffy. Add egg and blend well. Add flour, baking powder, baking soda and salt; mix well. Add remaining ingredients; stir just until blended. Spread dough onto a buttered 15"x10" jelly roll pan. Bake at 350 degrees for 20 to 25 minutes. Cool in pan on a wire rack; cut into squares when cool. Makes 3 dozen.

It's the perfect time of year to share some tasty treats
with teachers, librarians and school bus drivers...
let them know how much you appreciate them!

Harvest
for Sharing

Classic Snickerdoodle Cookies

*Becky Butler
Scroggins, TX*

I've been making this recipe for more than 30 years! These cookies come out perfectly crisp on the outside and chewy on the inside. In the fall, I often use freshly ground nutmeg instead of cinnamon for rolling the dough balls. The nutmeg lends a familiar yet unexpected flavor to the cookies that no one can resist! Having ingredients at room temperature really elevates your baking, so take the time to set out the eggs and butter.

1 c. butter, room temperature
1-3/4 c. sugar, divided
2 eggs, room temperature
2-1/2 c. all-purpose flour

2 t. cream of tartar
1 t. baking soda
1/4 t. salt
2 t. cinnamon or ground nutmeg

In a large bowl, beat butter and 1-1/2 cups sugar with an electric mixer on medium speed until fluffy. Add eggs, one at a time, beating until well combined; set aside. In another bowl, whisk together flour, cream of tartar, baking soda and salt. Add to butter mixture; stir just until combined. Combine remaining sugar and cinnamon or nutmeg in a shallow bowl; set aside. Shape dough into 1-1/4 inch balls; roll in cinnamon-sugar. Arrange on a parchment paper-lined baking sheet, about 2 inches apart. Bake at 375 degrees for 9 to 10 minutes, until golden and crinkly cracks appear. Cool on baking sheet for 2 to 3 minutes; remove to a wire rack and cool completely. Makes one dozen.

Parchment paper is a baker's best friend! Place it on a baking sheet to keep cookies from spreading and sticking. Clean-up is a breeze too. Generally, the paper can be reused at least once...when it starts to darken, toss it.

Scrumptious
Cookies & Desserts

Soft Ginger Cookies

Chelsea Davaine
Gheens, LA

*These cookies are my go-to recipe for fall and holiday baking.
They're quick & easy to make and everyone requests them
every time I make them. Give them a try!*

3/4 c. butter, softened
1 c. sugar
1 egg, beaten
1/4 c. molasses
2-1/4 c. all-purpose flour
1 t. baking soda

1/4 t. salt
2 t. ground ginger
3/4 t. cinnamon
1/2 t. ground cloves
Garnish: additional sugar

In a large bowl, beat butter and sugar until light and fluffy. Beat in egg
and molasses; set aside. In another bowl, combine flour, baking soda,
salt and spices. Gradually add flour mixture to butter mixture; mix well.
Roll dough into 1-1/2 inch balls; roll balls in sugar. Place on ungreased
baking sheets, 2 inches apart. Bake at 350 degrees for 10 to 12 minutes,
until puffy and lightly golden. Remove to wire racks to cool. Makes
2-1/2 dozen.

Cookies can be stored and still keep their just-baked taste up to
2 weeks. Just remember to keep them airtight...plastic zipping bags
or containers with tight-fitting lids are perfect. Even Grandma's
cookie jar will keep cookies delicious as long as the lid is on securely.

Harvest
for Sharing

Connie's Pumpkin Bars

Connie Neises
Overland Park, KS

This is the perfect recipe to feed a crowd for a tailgate party or simply at night for a cozy family dinner. I like to press a candy pumpkin or piece of candy corn into each square for added fall flair!

2 c. all-purpose flour
2 t. baking soda
1/2 t. salt
1 t. cinnamon
4 eggs, beaten

2 c. sugar
1 c. oil
15-oz. can pumpkin
1 c. chopped nuts

Combine all ingredients in a large bowl; mix well. Spread batter in a greased 15"x10" jelly-roll pan. Bake at 350 degrees for 30 to 35 minutes. Cool; spread with Cream Cheese Frosting and cut into bars. Makes 2 dozen.

Cream Cheese Frosting:

8-oz. pkg. cream cheese,
    room temperature
1/2 c. butter, room temperature

1 t. vanilla extract
2 c. powdered sugar

Beat together cream cheese and butter; mix in vanilla. Slowly beat in powdered sugar.

Keep a collection of colored sugars, candy sprinkles and edible glitter on hand. Sprinkle them on home-baked goodies...they'll be the hit of the next bake sale!

Scrumptious
Cookies & Desserts

Refrigerator Walnut Cookies

Judith Smith
Bellevue, WA

My mother always baked these delicious cookies during the fall and winter months. Everyone in the family enjoyed eating them.

1/2 c. butter, softened
1 c. brown sugar, packed
1 egg, beaten
3/4 t. salt

3/4 t. vanilla extract
1-1/2 c. all-purpose flour
1/2 t. baking soda
1/2 c. chopped walnuts

In a large bowl, combine butter, brown sugar, egg, salt and vanilla; beat until smooth and set aside. Mix flour and baking soda in a separate bowl; add to butter mixture and mix well. Fold in walnuts. Shape dough firmly into a roll, 2 inches in diameter. Wrap in 2 thicknesses of wax paper, twisting ends tightly. Chill in refrigerator for several hours or overnight. At baking time, slice dough into 1/8-inch slices; arrange on greased baking sheets. Bake at 375 degrees for 8 to 10 minutes, until edges are golden. Cool on wire racks. Makes about 2-1/2 dozen.

Stock up on your favorite nuts in the fall, when they're just-picked. Shelled or unshelled, nuts will stay fresher longer if they're stored in the freezer. As an added benefit, unshelled nuts will crack much easier when frozen.

Harvest
for Sharing

Pineapple Cookies

Holly Ann Flynn
Las Vegas, NV

My grandma was Italian and had a lot of grandchildren who loved her yummy frosted cookies, so she always made plenty!

6 eggs, beaten
16-oz. container shortening
2 c. sugar
2 t. vanilla extract

8 c. all-purpose flour
8 t. baking powder
20-oz. can crushed pineapple,
    drained and juice reserved

Combine eggs, shortening, sugar and vanilla in a very large bowl. Beat with an electric mixer on medium speed until blended. Gradually stir in flour, baking powder and pineapple. Drop dough by teaspoonfuls onto greased baking sheets. Bake at 400 degrees for 8 to 10 minutes. Cool on a wire rack; spread or drizzle with Frosting. Makes 8 dozen.

Frosting:

16-oz. pkg. powdered sugar
1 T. butter, softened

reserved pineapple juice

Stir together powdered sugar, butter and enough pineapple juice to make a thick icing or a thin glaze, as desired.

Take time to share family stories and traditions with your children. A cherished family recipe can be a great conversation starter.

Scrumptious
Cookies & Desserts

Yummy Apricot Bars

*Renee Spec
Crescent, PA*

These are a family favorite and just a little addictive...yum!

1-1/4 c. all-purpose flour
1/3 c. brown sugar, packed

1/2 c. butter, softened
3/4 c. apricot preserves

Combine flour, brown sugar and butter in a bowl; stir until crumbly. Press dough into a lightly greased 9"x9" baking pan. Bake at 350 degrees for 20 minutes. Spoon preserves over hot crust; spread to 1/2 inch from edges. Sprinkle evenly with Topping; bake another 25 minutes. When cool, cut into squares. Makes 1-1/4 dozen.

Topping:

3/4 c. flour
1/2 c. brown sugar, packed

1/4 c. butter, softened
1/2 t. almond extract

Combine all ingredients and mix well.

Invite girlfriends over for afternoon tea...a relaxing way to catch up! Have on hand yummy bite-size cookies and cakes along with finger sandwiches. Set out plenty of honey, lemon slices and half-and-half so everyone can have their tea just the way they like it.

Harvest
for Sharing

Jiffy Devil's Food Cake

Angie Mathews
Sabillasville, MD

This delicious chocolate cake recipe is from my mom. My children request it for every birthday and it is one of my favorites too...we all love it! It uses no eggs and is so easy to make. It makes great cupcakes and layer cakes, too. The Fluffy Chocolate Frosting is quick & easy to make...but this cake is even good with no frosting!

3 c. all-purpose flour
2 c. sugar
1 T. baking cocoa
1 t. salt
2 t. baking soda

2 T. vinegar
2/3 c. canola oil
2 t. vanilla extract
2 c. cold water

In a large bowl, combine flour, sugar, cocoa and salt; mix together and make a well in the center. Add baking soda and then vinegar to the well; mixture will bubble. Mix slightly. Add oil and vanilla; mix again. Slowly add cold water; beat until well blended, 2 to 3 minutes. Pour batter into a greased and floured 13"x9" baking pan. Bake at 350 degrees for 35 to 40 minutes, until a toothpick inserted in the center comes out clean. Remove from oven; set pan on a wire rack to cool. If desired, spread cooled cake with Fluffy Chocolate Frosting. Cut into squares and serve. Makes 12 to 15 servings.

Fluffy Chocolate Frosting:

3.9-oz. pkg. instant chocolate
    pudding mix
1 c. milk

8-oz. container frozen whipped
    topping, thawed

In a large bowl, beat pudding mix and milk for 2 minutes. Stir in whipped topping until well blended.

For blue-ribbon perfect chocolate
cakes with no white streaks, use
baking cocoa instead of flour
to dust greased pans.

Scrumptious
Cookies & Desserts

Perfectly Pleasing
Peanut Butter Pie

Cindy Slawski
Medford Lakes, NJ

This pie is a delicious and easy no-bake dessert for any festive fall gathering. We love it alongside the pumpkin and apple pies for Thanksgiving!

8-oz. container full-fat
    vanilla yogurt
8-oz. container frozen whipped
    topping, thawed
1/2 to 3/4 c. creamy
    peanut butter

9-inch chocolate graham cracker
    pie crust
2 peanut butter cups, chopped
Optional: chocolate sauce,
    additional whipped topping

In a large bowl, combine yogurt and whipped topping. Stir well with a wooden spoon; set aside. In a microwave-safe cup, microwave desired amount of peanut butter for 20 to 30 seconds, until melted enough to stir. Whisk into whipped topping mixture. Spread mixture evenly in pie crust; sprinkle chopped peanut butter cups over pie. Drizzle with chocolate sauce, if desired. Cover and freeze. Before serving, let stand at room temperature for 20 to 30 minutes. Cut into wedges; top with dollops of whipped topping for a fancier look, if desired. Makes 8 servings.

For the easiest fireside treats ever, round up an assortment of ingredients for s'mores...graham crackers, chocolate-coated cookies, fun-size candy bars and peanut butter cups.
Don't forget the marshmallows!

Harvest
for Sharing

Pumpkin-Chocolate Chip Cookies
Jill Keaton
Fort Worth, TX

This is my son's favorite recipe. Every time friends come to visit, they ask for these cookies, no matter the season.

1 c. butter, softened
1 c. light brown sugar, packed
1 c. sugar
1 egg, beaten
1 t. vanilla extract
1 c. canned pumpkin
2-1/2 c. all-purpose flour

1 c. rolled oats, uncooked
1 t. baking powder
1 t. cinnamon
1/2 t. salt
1/2 c. chopped walnuts
1 c. semi-sweet chocolate chips

In a large bowl, beat butter and sugars until fluffy. Beat in egg, vanilla and pumpkin; set aside. In a separate bowl, mix together remaining ingredients. Stir flour mixture into pumpkin mixture, a little at a time, until well combined. Drop dough by heaping teaspoonfuls onto parchment paper-lined baking sheets. Bake at 350 degrees for 15 to 20 minutes, until lightly golden around the edges. Makes 4 dozen.

One of the best ways to give thanks is to help someone else.
Volunteer, lend a neighbor a hand, leave a surprise on someone's
doorstep...there are lots of thoughtful ways to show you care.

Scrumptious
Cookies & Desserts

Kimberly's Mexican Chocolate Fudge

Kimberly Redeker
Savoy, IL

I love the warmth of Mexican chocolate...it's not spicy, just a simple flavor that warms you like a hug! This fudge is based on my mom's basic fudge recipe. I call this borrowing a classic and making it generational. Thank you, Mom, for all the memories of making fudge in your kitchen!

1/2 c. butter
12-oz. can evaporated milk
4 c. sugar
1 T. vanilla extract
1 t. almond extract
1 T. cinnamon

1-1/2 t. cayenne pepper
1-1/2 t. ground ginger
10-oz. pkg. mini marshmallows
12-oz. pkg. semi-sweet
    chocolate chips
Garnish: additional cinnamon

Melt butter in a large heavy saucepan over medium heat. Add evaporated milk, sugar, extracts and spices; bring to a boil. Cook and stir over medium heat, stirring constantly, until mixture reaches the soft-ball stage, or 234 to 243 degrees on a candy thermometer. Remove from heat. Rapidly stir in marshmallows and chocolate chips. Pour into a buttered 14"x11" jelly-roll pan; let cool. Sprinkle with cinnamon; cut into squares. Makes 12 dozen pieces.

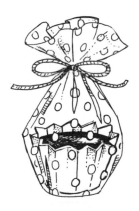

Yum...super-size fudge cups! Just spoon warm fudge into foil muffin cups. Wrap individually in squares of colorful cellophane. Perfect for gifting!

Harvest
for Sharing

Fall Harvest Pie

Paula Marchesi
Auburn, PA

To me, fall is the best time of the year, with cool weather and lots of fruits and veggies to bake, cook up and freeze. If you like, make this pie all with just apples or just pears. I serve this often and very rarely have any leftovers. It goes well for Thanksgiving, when I serve this with a pumpkin pie.

9-inch pie crust, unbaked
1/2 c. pure maple syrup
2 T. all-purpose flour
2 T. butter, melted
2-1/2 c. Granny Smith apples, peeled, cored and sliced
2-1/2 c. Bartlett pears, cored and sliced
1 c. fresh or frozen cranberries
Optional: ice cream or whipped cream

Line a 9" pie plate with pie crust. Trim and flute edges; set aside. In a large bowl, mix maple syrup, flour and melted butter until smooth. Add apples, pears, and cranberries; mix gently and spoon into crust. Sprinkle Topping over filling. Cover edges of crust loosely with aluminum foil to prevent overbrowning. Bake at 400 for 15 minutes; reduce heat to 350 degrees. Remove foil; bake for 35 to 40 minutes longer, until filling is bubbly and crust is golden. Cool pie on a wire rack. Cut into wedges; serve topped with ice cream or whipped cream, if desired. Makes 6 to 8 servings.

Topping:

1/2 c. all-purpose flour
1/4 c. brown sugar, packed
1 t. cinnamon
1/3 c. cold butter, cubed
1/2 c. chopped walnuts

Combine flour, brown sugar and cinnamon; cut in butter until crumbly. Stir in walnuts.

Good apple pies are a considerable part of our happiness.

–Jane Austen

Scrumptious
Cookies & Desserts

Apple Cookies

Lynnette Jones
East Flat Rock, NC

The county we live in has lots of apple farmers, so there is a Labor Day Apple Festival celebration. There are week-long activities, with the weekend filled with vendors selling apples and apple products. So when I think of fall, I think apples!

1/2 c. shortening
1 c. light brown sugar, packed
1 egg, beaten
1-1/2 c. all-purpose flour
1/2 t. baking soda
1/2 t. salt

1/2 t. nutmeg
1/2 t. cinnamon
1 c. Honey Crisp or Golden
    Delicious apple, cored
    and chopped

In a large bowl, beat shortening, brown sugar and egg until light and fluffy. Stir in flour, baking soda, salt and spices; fold in apple. Drop dough by teaspoonfuls onto greased or parchment paper-lined baking sheets. Bake at 375 degrees for 8 to 10 minutes, until lightly golden. Makes 2 dozen.

If you're pressed for time, mix up cookie dough, pop it
in the refrigerator, and bake later when guests arrive.
They'll love arriving to the aroma of fresh-baked cookies!

Harvest
for Sharing

Rocky Road Candy

Bev Traxler
British Columbia, Canada

A melt-in-your-mouth combination of chocolate, peanuts and marshmallows...one of my favorites. Freezes well, but it's doubtful you'll have any left to freeze!

6-oz. pkg. semi-sweet
   chocolate chips
1-oz. sq. unsweetened
   baking chocolate
1 T. butter
2 eggs

1-1/4 c. powdered sugar
1/2 t. salt
1 t. vanilla extract
2 c. mini marshmallows
2 c. salted peanuts

Melt chocolate chips, baking chocolate and butter in a large heavy saucepan over low heat, stirring until smooth. Remove from heat. In a bowl, beat eggs until foamy; mix in powdered sugar, salt and vanilla. Blend in chocolate mixture; stir in marshmallows and peanuts. Drop mixture by teaspoonfuls onto wax paper-lined baking sheets. Chill for 2 hours, or until firm. Store in refrigerator; remove just before serving. Makes about 4 dozen.

Someone special would love to receive their very own cookie & candy assortment. Tuck small cookies and squares of fudge into mini paper muffin liners...arrange in separate compartments of a candy box. Sweet!

Scrumptious
Cookies & Desserts

Chocolate Caramel Bars

Coleen Lambert
Luxemburg, WI

Everyone has these four ingredients and 20 minutes...this is way too easy! My grandkids make these scrumptious bars all the time.

1 c. all-purpose flour
3/4 c. brown sugar, packed
   and divided

1/4 c. plus 1/3 c. butter, divided
1/2 c. semi-sweet chocolate chips

In a bowl, combine flour, 1/2 cup brown sugar and 1/4 cup butter. Mix with 2 forks until crumbly. Press into the bottom of a greased 8"x8" glass baking pan; set aside. Melt remaining butter in a small saucepan over medium heat; stir in remaining brown sugar. Bring to a boil; boil for one minute. Remove from heat; spoon over crust. Bake at 350 degrees for 15 minutes. Do not overbake! Remove from oven. Sprinkle with chocolate chips; swirl with a knife. Let cool; cut into bars. Makes one dozen.

Black Forest Brownies

Gladys Kielar
Whitehouse, OH

A delicious dessert that's ready to enjoy in almost no time.

18-oz. pkg. brownie mix
21-oz. can cherry pie filling
1/2 c. oil

2 eggs, beaten
1-1/4 c. semi-sweet
   chocolate chips

Grease the bottom of a 13"x9" baking pan; set aside. In a large bowl, mix dry brownie mix, pie filling, oil and eggs; pour batter into pan. Bake at 350 degrees for 30 to 35 minutes, testing with a toothpick. Immediately sprinkle chocolate chips evenly over brownies; spread when melted. Let cool; cut into squares. Makes one dozen.

Use a plastic knife to cut brownies,
for a clean cut every time.

Harvest
for Sharing

Lizzie's Own Cookies

Liz Osterholt
Celina, OH

This is an original recipe that I've been making at Thanksgiving for more than 30 years. Filled with fruit and nuts, they're best if they are aged for a few weeks, so you may want to plan ahead.

1-1/2 c. raisins
1/4 c. bourbon or orange juice
1/4 c. butter
1/2 c. brown sugar, packed
2 eggs, beaten
1-1/2 c. all-purpose flour
1-1/2 t. baking soda

3/4 t. cinnamon
1/4 t. nutmeg
1/4 t. ground cloves
1/2 lb. pecan halves
1/2 lb. candied cherries
1/4 lb. candied citron, diced

In a small bowl, stir together raisins and bourbon or orange juice; let stand for one hour. Meanwhile, stir butter in another bowl until soft. Beat in brown sugar and then eggs; set aside. In a separate bowl, sift flour, baking soda and spices. Add to butter mixture and stir well. Add raisin mixture, pecans, cherries and citron; mix well. Drop dough by teaspoonfuls onto greased baking sheets, one inch apart. Bake at 325 degrees for about 15 minutes. Let cool; store in an airtight container in a cool, dry place. Flavor improves if aged for several weeks. May be frozen. Makes 6 dozen.

Stir up some Grizzly Gorp for snacking and tucking into lunchboxes. Just toss together 2 cups bear-shaped graham crackers, one cup mini marshmallows, one cup peanuts and 1/2 cup seedless raisins. Yum!

Scrumptious
Cookies & Desserts

Penuche Coconuts

Stephanie Nilsen
Fremont, NE

One of Mom's go-to recipes for cookies...they are crispy and chewy and yummy! Mom always made sure the cookie jar was filled.

1 c. shortening	2 c. all-purpose flour
2 c. brown sugar, packed	1/2 t. salt
1 t. vanilla extract	1 t. baking soda
2 eggs, beaten	8-oz. pkg. flaked coconut

In a large bowl, beat shortening and brown sugar; add vanilla. Add eggs, one at a time, beating well after each; set aside. In another bowl, sift together flour, salt and baking soda; add to shortening mixture and blend well. Stir in coconut. Drop dough by teaspoonfuls onto ungreased baking sheets, 2 inches apart. Bake at 375 degrees for 8 to 10 minutes. Cool slightly on pans; remove to a wire rack to finish cooling. Makes about 4 dozen.

Send homemade cookies to college students so they arrive just before final exams...a sure-fire way to make them smile.

White Chocolate Chip Lemon Cookies

Nancy Kaiser
York, SC

If you like lemon, you will love these cookies! They're a nice change from rich fall flavors like pumpkin and chocolate.

2 c. all-purpose flour
3/4 t. baking soda
1/2 t. salt
3/4 c. butter, softened
1/2 c. brown sugar, packed
1/4 c. sugar

1 egg
2 t. lemon zest
2 T. lemon juice
1 c. white chocolate chips
Optional: 1 c. chopped walnuts

Combine flour, baking soda and salt in a bowl; set aside. In a separate large bowl, beat butter and sugars; beat in egg, lemon zest and juice. Gradually beat in flour mixture; stir in remaining ingredients. Using a 2-ounce scoop, drop dough onto ungreased baking sheets. Bake at 375 degrees for 10 to 12 minutes, until edges are lightly golden. Makes 3 to 4 dozen.

Cooler weather and longer evenings are a cozy time just right for curling up with a good book. Keep several of your favorites on a table next to a cozy chair...brew a cup of spiced tea and sit back to enjoy.

Scrumptious
Cookies & Desserts

Grandma Penny's Lemon Cake

Leslie Harvie
Simpsonville, SC

My sweet grandma preferred shopping to baking, but she did enjoy making this cake. We often enjoyed a slice together after a long day at the mall.

3-oz. pkg. lemon gelatin mix
3/4 c. boiling water
15-1/4 oz. pkg. white cake mix
3/4 c. oil

4 eggs, beaten
1 T. lemon extract
1 t. almond extract

In a large bowl, dissolve gelatin mix in boiling water. Let mixture cool; stir in dry cake mix and oil. Add eggs, one at a time, beating well after each addition. Stir in extracts. Pour batter into a greased and floured tube pan. Bake at 325 degrees for 40 to 45 minutes. Cool in pan for several minutes; turn cake out onto a serving plate and cool. Serves 12 to 16.

Whip up a jolly Jack-o'-Lantern shake! In a blender, combine 3 scoops vanilla ice cream, 1/4 cup milk, 2 tablespoons canned pumpkin and 1/4 teaspoon pumpkin pie spice. Blend until smooth. Pour into tall glasses and share with a friend.

Quick Apple Dumplings

Barbara Doggett
Pulaski, TN

I had never heard of apple dumplings until a lady fixed these for an event at church. I tasted one and I was hooked! They are so good.

2 Granny Smith apples, peeled, cored and quartered
8-oz. tube refrigerated crescent rolls, separated
1/8 t. cinnamon
1/2 c. butter

1 c. sugar
1 c. orange juice
1 t. vanilla extract
1/2 c. pecans, very finely chopped

Wrap each apple quarter in a crescent roll. Arrange in a greased 8"x8" baking pan; sprinkle with cinnamon and set aside. Combine butter, sugar and orange juice in a saucepan over medium heat; bring to a boil. Remove from heat; stir in vanilla and spoon over dumplings. Sprinkle pecans on top. Bake at 350 degrees for 30 minutes, or until crust is golden and apples are just fork-tender. To serve, spoon syrup from pan over dumplings. Makes 8 servings.

Warm caramel ice cream topping makes a delightful drizzle over Quick Apple Dumplings. Just heat it in the microwave for a few seconds, and it's ready to spoon over desserts.

Scrumptious
Cookies & Desserts

Grandma Kropp's Raisin Pie

Josiah Kropp
Boiling Springs, SC

This is my dad's favorite pie that his grandma used to make it all the time. It is her secret recipe that no other raisin pie can beat...simple, but delicious.

2 c. raisins
3/4 c. sugar
3 T. cornstarch

1/4 c. water
1 T. lemon juice
2 9-inch pie crusts, unbaked

Add raisins to a saucepan; add enough water to cover just above raisins. Bring to a boil over medium heat. Reduce heat to medium-low; simmer for about 15 minutes, until raisins are plump. Stir in sugar; simmer until sugar is dissolved. Mix cornstarch and 1/4 cup water in a cup; add to pan. Cook and stir until clear and thick. Remove from heat; stir in lemon juice. Arrange one crust in a 9" pie plate; spoon raisin mixture into crust. Add top crust; flute edges, pinch to seal and cut steam vents. Bake at 425 degrees for 30 to 35 minutes, until crust is golden. Cool; cut into wedges and serve. Makes 6 servings.

Celebrate the spooky season...surround an orange pillar candle with candy corn in a glass hurricane.

217

INDEX

Appetizers

Artichoke Bruschetta, 172
Autumn Chicken Salad Spread, 174
Autumn Snack Mix, 178
Bacon-Wrapped Avocados, 149
Baked Potato Dip, 153
Cheesy Pull-Aparts, 147
Chris's Homemade Salsa, 162
Easy Pepper Jelly Appetizer, 169
Easy Queso Dip, 176
Fall Corn Fritters, 164
Fresh Pico de Gallo, 149
Fried Olives, 161
Fried Pickles, 161
Game-Day Buffalo Wings, 165
Garlic Filling Stuffed Bread, 156
Layered Hummus Dip, 163
Mini Bacon-Ranch Cheese Balls, 173
Mushroom Mozzarella Bruschetta, 154
Oven-Fried Sesame Chicken Wings, 157
Parmesan Chicken Brochettes, 150
Pizza Popcorn Spice Mix, 167
Pricketts' Pumpkins Farm-Roasted
  Seeds, 178
Pumpkin Spice Hummus, 168
Santa Fe Rice, 177
Sausage & Cream Cheese Wraps, 155
Spicy Party Mix, 167
Stuffed Artie-Chokes, 160
Sunday Cheese Sticks, 152
Super Bowl of Beer Cheese, 159
Tailgate Dip, 153
Toffee Caramel Apple Dip, 168
Walking Tacos, 148
Wonderful Corn Dip, 146

Beverages

Apple Cider Refresher, 175
Cranberry Lemonade, 175
Easy Coffee Punch, 28
Easy Tailgating Punch, 172
Farmers' Hot Spiced Tomato Juice, 177
Hot Spiced Cider, 159
Spiced Tea with Ginger, 15

Breads

Apple Butter Bread, 27
Apple Pie Monkey Bread, 26
Back-to-School Bread, 73
Bacon-Cheddar Bread, 77
Blueberry Bread, 18
Corny Raisin Muffins, 81
Dilly Bread, 89
Heloisa's Oat Muffins, 21
Herb Biscuit Knots, 95
Homestead Oatmeal Bread, 103
Oats & Cereal Flatbread, 91
Pecan Pie Muffins, 31
Pineapple Cornmeal Muffins, 104
Pumpkin Patch Biscuits, 97
Pumpkin Spice Muffins, 11
Southern Buttermilk Cornbread, 93
Special Herb Butter, 85
Vicky's Easy Homemade Bread, 85
Yogurt Biscuits, 29

Breakfasts

Apple Cider Doughnuts, 16
Aunt Carol's Sour Cream Coffee Cake, 8
Autumn Oat Bars, 11
Bacon & Egg Breakfast Cupcakes, 33
Baked Eggs & 4 Cheeses, 19
Banana-Nut Baked Oatmeal, 22
Breakfast Burritos, 14
Brown Sugar Baked Oatmeal, 24
Cast-Iron Skillet Loaded Breakfast
  Biscuits, 10
Coffee Shop Egg Bites, 7
Dark Chocolate-Cranberry Granola Bars,
  35
French Toast Strata Pie, 23
Game-Day Breakfast Casserole, 28
Grandma George's Onion Gravy &
  Biscuits, 36
Harvest Breakfast Casserole, 34
Italian Ham & Egg Bake, 32
Light & Crispy Waffles, 12
Mini Muffin Doughnuts, 15
Mom's Sweet Potato Waffles, 6
Overnight Egg Bake, 16
Puffy Pancake with Fruit, 25
Quick & Easy Cinnamon Buns, 25
Skillet Apples, 13
Stuffed French Toast, 17
Tex-Mex Egg & Potato Skillet, 9
Velvet's Weekend Frittata, 20
Verna's Superior Pancakes, 30

INDEX

Candies

Kimberly's Mexican Chocolate
  Fudge, 207
Maple-Nut Popcorn, 170
Rocky Road Candy, 210
Sally's Oven Caramel Corn, 171

Cookies

Apple Cookies, 209
Best-Ever Brownies, 189
Black Forest Brownies, 211
Butterscotch Crispy Rice Treats, 193
Buttery Spiced Walnut Cookies, 183
Chocolate Caramel Bars, 211
Classic Snickerdoodle Cookies, 198
Coconut-Honey Bars, 197
Connie's Pumpkin Bars, 200
Easy Monster Cookies, 195
Great-Grandma Walling's Sugar
  Cookies, 184
Lizzie's Own Cookies, 212
Maple No-Bake Cookies, 193
Parker's Sneaky Chocolate Chip
  Cookies, 182
Penuche Coconuts, 213
Pineapple Cookies, 202
Pumpkin-Chocolate Chip Cookies, 206
Refrigerator Walnut Cookies, 201
School Cafeteria Peanut Butter Bars, 188
Soft Ginger Cookies, 199
Spiced Apple Butter Bars, 192
Toffee Graham Treats, 192
White Chocolate Chip Lemon
  Cookies, 214
Yummy Apricot Bars, 203

Desserts

Any Day's a Party Ice Cream Cake, 181
Aunt Edna's Sweet Potato Pies, 187
Baked Indian Pudding, 191
Caramel Apple Crumble, 190
Fall Harvest Pie, 208
Grandma Kropp's Raisin Pie, 217
Grandma Penny's Lemon Cake, 215
Happy Birthday Cake, 194
Jiffy Devil's Food Cake, 204
Mama's Pumpkin Pie, 186

Oh-So-Good Apple Pie, 180
Pear Bundt Cake, 186
Perfectly Pleasing Peanut Butter Pie, 205
Pineapple-Cranberry Cake, 196
Pumpkin Eclair Cake, 185
Quick Apple Dumplings, 216

Mains

Ann's Baked Ham, 119
Artichoke Spaghetti, 110
Autumn Fiesta Chicken Casserole, 106
Back-to-School Baby Back Ribs, 133
Baja-Style Chicken Bowls, 109
Baked Cavatini, 111
Cabbage & Brats Skillet, 118
Cabbage Casserole, 143
Cafe-Style Pinto Beans, 133
Cheese-Filled Manicotti, 120
Cheesy Tuna Noodle Casserole, 123
Chicken with Dijon-Cranberry
  Sauce, 115
Corn Chip Bake, 127
Dutch Oven Parmesan Chicken, 113
Easy Chili Con Carne, 109
Enchilada Casserole, 142
Family-Favorite Beer Sausage, 129
Gigi's Thanksgiving Turkey &
  Gravy, 114
Kielbasa & Cabbage, 107
Leftover Turkey Dinner Casserole, 138
Lemon Herbed Chicken, 139
Lemony Fish Roll-Ups, 134
Mama Simpson's Spaghetti Bake, 121
Milwaukee Pork Stew, 136
Mom's Classic Meatloaf, 108
Mother's Shrimp Puff, 135
Mr. Payne's Beef Enchiladas, 132
Oven Bar-B-Que Chicken, 128
Provence Pork, 139
Sassy Salsa Chicken, 117
Shrimp & Grits, 122
Shrimp Noodle Bowls, 135
Silly String Pie, 144
Slow-Cooker Bourbon Chicken, 137
Slow-Cooker Italian Chicken &
  Noodles, 125
Slow-Cooker Pot Roast, 116
Slow-Cooker Salisbury Meatballs, 141

INDEX

Slow-Cooker Spiced Cider Pork Loin, 130
Smoked Sausage & Bowties, 129
Smothered Pork Chops, 131
Super-Easy Chicken Cacciatore, 112
Taco Tuesday Chicken Pasta Bake, 126
Turkey Tamale Bake, 124
Ziti Pizza Casserole, 140

Salads

Autumn Harvest Pasta Salad, 38
Broccoli & Bacon Salad, 39
Cranberry Waldorf Gelatin Salad, 58
Creamy Fruit Salad, 59
Crisp & Easy Apple Salad, 41
Easy Vegetable Salad, 52
Favorite Broccoli Salad, 53
German Potato Salad, 68
Grandma Joan's Taco Salad, 46
Honey-Mustard Coleslaw with
    Apples, 41
Make & Take Mac Salad, 69
Mom's Party Salad, 64
Romaine & Pear Salad, 40
Sauerkraut Slaw, 65
Vicki's Linguine & Veggie Salad, 47

Sandwiches

Grandma's Roast Italian Beef, 158
Hot Crusty Picnic Loaf, 166
Mississippi Chicken Sandwiches, 151

Sides

3-Cheese Macaroni & Cheese, 45
Apple Chestnut Stuffing, 48
Baked Acorn Squash with Cinnamon
    Apples, 43
Barley Mushroom Casserole, 67
Butternut Squash Jumble, 56
Cheesy Oniony Hashbrown
    Casserole, 44
Cornbread Zucchini Bake, 62
Cranberry Baked Beans, 57
Cranberry-Orange Sauce, 67
Creamy Cheesy Scalloped Potatoes, 54
German Green Beans, 51

Grandma Dee's Dressing, 60
Grandmother's Molasses Baked
    Beans, 57
Green Chile Corn Soufflé, 42
Homestyle Mashed Potatoes, 63
Joyce's Squash Casserole, 55
Loretta's Yams, 70
Luscious Onion Casserole, 50
Mom's Zucchini Casserole, 63
Parmesan Baked Potatoes, 51
Roasted Pears & Sweet Potatoes, 61
Stuffed Artichoke Casserole, 49
Wild Rice with Orange Juice &
    Cranberries, 66

Soups

Alphabet Soup, 72
Best Cheese Soup, 75
Broccoli-Cheddar Potato Soup, 102
Cheesy Chicken & Vegetable Soup, 79
Cheesy Potato Soup, 101
Colors of Fall Soup, 84
Courtney's Creamy Tomato Tortellini
    Soup, 76
Creamy Corn Chowder, 99
Creamy Italian Bean Soup, 87
Crystal's Vegetarian Egg Drop Soup, 78
David's Taco Soup, 99
Fiesta Chicken Soup, 92
Hamburger Soup, 83
Harvest Black Bean & Pumpkin Chili, 80
Jordan's Scarecrow Chili, 74
Lori's Fall Chowder, 96
Mom's 7-Can Soup, 82
Pantry Chili, 75
Pumpkin Spice Bisque, 104
Quick Chicken Posole, 100
Quick White Chicken Chili, 95
Roasted Garlic Soup, 88
Smashed Potato Soup, 90
Tasty Beef & Vegetable Soup, 94
Turkey, Dressing & Dumpling Soup, 98
Unstuffed Cabbage Soup, 78
Zucchini & Italian Sausage Soup, 86

Find Gooseberry Patch
wherever you are!

www.gooseberrypatch.com

Email

Call us toll-free at 1·800·854·6673

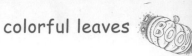

homecoming parades colorful leaves

casual get-togethers

drives in the country

moonlit hayrides

craft fairs

community suppers crackling bonfires

U.S. to Metric Recipe Equivalents

Volume Measurements

1/4 teaspoon	1 mL
1/2 teaspoon	2 mL
1 teaspoon	5 mL
1 tablespoon = 3 teaspoons	15 mL
2 tablespoons = 1 fluid ounce	30 mL
1/4 cup	60 mL
1/3 cup	75 mL
1/2 cup = 4 fluid ounces	125 mL
1 cup = 8 fluid ounces	250 mL
2 cups = 1 pint =16 fluid ounces	500 mL
4 cups = 1 quart	1 L

Weights

1 ounce	30 g
4 ounces	120 g
8 ounces	225 g
16 ounces = 1 pound	450 g

Oven Temperatures

300° F	150° C
325° F	160° C
350° F	180° C
375° F	190° C
400° F	200° C
450° F	230° C

Baking Pan Sizes

Square	
8x8x2 inches	2 L = 20x20x5 cm
9x9x2 inches	2.5 L = 23x23x5 cm
Rectangular	
13x9x2 inches	3.5 L = 33x23x5 cm

Loaf	
9x5x3 inches	2 L = 23x13x7 cm
Round	
8x1-1/2 inches	1.2 L = 20x4 cm
9x1-1/2 inches	1.5 L = 23x4 cm